The Human Drama behind
the Walker Spy Case

# Daughter
## OF
# Deceit

## Laura Walker

### With Jerry Horner

WORD PUBLISHING
Dallas · London · Sydney · Singapore

Unless otherwise specified, Scripture quotations are from The Living Bible, copyright 1971 by Tyndale House Publishers, Wheaton, Ill. Used by permission. References to J. B. Philips refer to The New Testament in Modern English by J. B. Phillips, published by The Macmillan Company, © 1958, 1960, 1972 by J. B. Phillips. Those referred to by NASB are from the New American Standard Bible, copyright © The Lockman Foundation 1960, 1962, 1963, 1968, 1971, 1972, 1973, 1975, 1977.

Library of Congress Cataloging-in-Publication Data

Walker, Laura, 1960–
    Daughter of deceit : the human drama behind the Walker spy case /
Laura Walker with Jerry Horner.
        p.    cm.
    ISBN 0-8499-0659-8
    1. Walker, Laura, 1960–   .  2. Christian biography—United
States.  3. Walker, John Anthony, 1937–   .  4. Walker family.
5. Espionage—Soviet Union—History—20th century.  6. Espionage—
United States—History—20th century.  I. Horner, Jerry, 1936–
II. Title.
BR1725.W285A3  1988
327.1′2′0922—dc19                                          88-27546
[B]                                                              CIP

8 9 8 0 1 2 3 9  AGK  9 8 7 6 5 4 3 2 1

Printed in the United States of America

To Chris
whose love has healed
the pain of separation.

# Contents

6 *Contents*

# Foreword

June 18, 1985, was one of those sun-drenched days that encourages people to sneak away from the office early, and the temptation was irresistible to me. There would be plenty of time for the family to enjoy a late swim at Indian Cove, followed by a cookout. The afternoon repeat of the morning's telecast of the "700 Club" played to an empty room as we busied ourselves with preparations for the outing. Everything was finally ready, and the rest of the household headed for the car while I went into the family room to click off the television.

Two minutes can be an eternity to an impatient five-year-old boy. That much time elapsed before my son, Thad, returned in a huff to demand that I leave with them. That's not exactly how he put it, but he got his point across anyway. My response of "in a minute" didn't convince him, especially since he noticed my interest in the interview being aired at that moment. Questioning my sense of values at making Indian Cove wait in preference to watching two women talk to each other, he returned outside to report on the delay.

The two women were Danuta Soderman, cohost of the "700 Club," and a guest, Laura Walker Snyder, daughter of the celebrated Navy spy, John Walker, whose case was still front-page news. I sat captivated by what I saw and heard. Much later I learned that Pat Robertson, having screened the taped interview, ordered Laura's identity and background thoroughly checked before he permitted the program to be shown. He felt that she was an actress rather than the daughter of the man who had just been arrested for espionage, the charges based primarily on the information provided by the daughter. She was pretty, poised, and composed, and didn't stumble once during the interview.

7

I could well understand Pat's skepticism, but the young woman was indeed who she claimed to be, and the story that she briefly reviewed was electrifying. The next day's telecast, when she appeared live with her five-year-old son, packed an even greater punch. Inexplicably, I sensed that I would have some contact with this woman, but I had no idea in what capacity.

Within three weeks the personnel department of CBN forwarded to me a job application that Laura had submitted. It so happened that the faculty of CBN University's School of Biblical Studies, of which I served as dean, was in need of an additional secretary. After interviewing her and determining that she met the necessary qualifications, I notified her that she could begin her new position on July 22. In January 1986 she became my personal secretary.

In the three years that she has been employed under my supervision, I have come to know this beautiful stout-hearted young woman as few have, observing on a daily basis her strengths and weaknesses, her highs and lows. Besides our professional relationship, she and her son, Chris, who is the same age as our Thad, are frequent guests in our home. The two boys are solid friends, and Chris often stays overnight with us.

The three years since her father's arrest have not been easy for Laura, but, as disclosed in this book, most all of her years have been difficult. Recent years have been beneficial for her, though, as a time of discipline in the process of spiritual and emotional maturation. When I first met her she had no resources and owned nothing except a few articles of clothing. Starting from that zero base she was responsible for securing housing and furnishings, transportation, and daily sustenance for herself and her son with only a gaunt salary to support her. During most of the time I have known her, she has worked at a second job.

She met this challenge with the same tenacity that had toughened her survival instincts during years of stern combat with adversities that struck hard and often and which demanded far more than physical prowess to overcome them.

She has suffered reversals, and her faith has faltered. Often I have had to postpone dictation in favor of counsel and prayer with her. At such times, God has always proved Himself faithful.

Laura has never reveled in her celebrity status, and all she has desired is to provide a home for her son, which is actually the untold part of the story surrounding the breaking of the most damaging spy ring in this country's history. Although several books have been written on the case, each one contains numerous inaccuracies and none has been written from the perspective of a Walker family member, particularly the one whose search for her son was primarily responsible for the exposure of John Walker and his associates. In addition, a forthcoming television miniseries about the Walker family is a horrible distortion of the characters, written by imaginative writers who know little about the people they are portraying. For the most part, the script is gross fabrication. Such falsehoods have distressed Laura immensely, and she is concerned that the public know the true facts of the family and the case.

This story could have been told differently, highlighting certain incidents that are shocking but at the same time titillating. Laura, however, has chosen to glorify grace more than sin. One publisher breached a contract with her when she refused to write the book in a manner that would feature the obscene and the profane. We therefore express sincere gratitude to Word Books for allowing her to present her story in her way.

If it is anything at all, this book is a message of hope, assuring the abused and downtrodden that there is a divine deliverer in whom they can trust and upon whom they can rely for help. What she offers is more than religious platitudes and holy shibboleths. She offers instead her experience. Like Abraham, she believed "in hope against hope."

Jerry Horner
Virginia Beach, Virginia
June 1988

# Introduction

As I write these words, I am only twenty-eight years of age, but I have lived at least three lifetimes. I gained a notoriety of sorts as the betrayer of a betrayer, when, along with my mother, I gave the FBI information that brought to a conclusion the activities of the most successful spy in America's history, both in terms of longevity and the amount and value of sensitive material delivered to his employers. The fact that the master spy was my own father added to the sensational nature of the news, and I suddenly was catapulted from the streets where I had been living into the studios of the major television talk shows.

The response to my role in the case of John Walker was immediate and varied. I was caught in a "damned if I do, damned if I don't" situation, and the critics were evenly divided. Many people castigated me for not pulling the plug on my father years earlier, when I first learned of his espionage activities. Some of them even suggested that I should share my father's punishment. Others accused me of being the lowest kind of informer for giving the Judas kiss to my father, and "rat fink" was one of the more complimentary terms.

Still others have charged that I exploited the situation, capitalizing on my notoriety for gain. It is true that I appeared many times on various television programs, but there was little or no remuneration for each appearance. Additionally, I rejected lucrative offers from glossy smut magazines and supermarket exposé tabloids, and they were numerous.

Several books and multitudinous articles have been written about the Walker spy case, but not one has given adequate consideration to the events leading up to the exposure of the espionage ring. All the attention has been focused on my father, on his surveillance by the FBI in breaking the case,

11

and on the irreparable damage done to the security of
the United States. The story has not been told from the
perspective of any Walker family member, particularly my
own, which is of special significance in light of the fact that
it was my experiences which ultimately led to John Walker's
downfall. Furthermore, other publications have no small
number of inaccuracies and fabrications, especially when
dealing with family matters.

This book, then, is not my father's story; it is mine. It
relates some events that are shamefully disgraceful, and the
honest straightforwardness with which they have been
described has been both painful and humiliating. There was a
strong temptation to yield to profitable offers to present this
story in a lurid manner that would emphasize the more earthy
features of my life, but I have no desire to glorify immoral
principles. I wanted to tell my own story in my own way, and
I'm grateful to the publishers for allowing me to do so.

Others, particularly my mother, will suffer embarrassment
from the contents of this book, but they will not be able to
plead innocence. My father will be unaffected because he
left feelings behind years ago. What I have written lacks
the venom of a vindictive spirit and the bitter flavor of
resentment. The harsh things reported about my parents
are told with simple candidness in order to explain their part
in shaping the life that I had in contrast to what I have
become. I love my family and pass judgment on no one. I
have tried to relate only what happened.

Discussing this book with other family members has drawn
my siblings and me closer together and has brought to all of
us a clearer understanding of our mother. It is the beginning
of a process of healing old wounds, long scabbed over but
left untreated. I have had no communication at all with my
father since his arrest. Since the news broke concerning the
breakup of the spy ring headed by my father, and my part in
it, hundreds of questions have been directed at me. Most of
them are asked out of curiosity, many are dripping with
venom, and others reflect genuine concern.

The most frequently asked questions are: Why did you blow the whistle on your father? Why did you wait so long? How do you feel about it now? Do you regret betraying your father, especially since your brother and your uncle were also involved? Has your life been affected? Would you do the same thing again? How did your family react? What is your relationship with your family now, especially your father? These matters are all addressed in this volume.

Throughout the writing of this book, I was careful to give conscious effort to telling a story to which people could relate. I do not offer accounts of sensational, instantaneous miracles or prescribe shortcuts to success. I have traveled a torturous road, and thousands of people will recognize themselves in my company—people who have suffered the anguish of parental rejection, the brutality of physical and emotional abuse, the humiliation of rape, the loneliness of abandonment, the horridness of living on the streets, the grief of drugs, the stigma of attempted suicide, the wretchedness of a miserable marriage, the distress of suddenly losing a child by a treacherous kidnapping and the subsequent heartache of years of wondering, of longing to see him, of desiring to touch him or to hear his voice. If it is true that misery loves company, then my sphere of existence has been drastically overcrowded.

My purpose in confessing such sorrows, however, is not to spew curses upon those who have wronged me. Nor is it to sit in the circle of Job's comforters. My foremost desire is to assure people who have identified with my experiences that there is strength for their weakness and deliverance from their hopelessness. Even the smallest light is greatly appreciated in the deepest darkness. If this book ignites but one spark of hope, then the pain it has cost me will be a small price to pay.

Laura Walker
Virginia Beach, Virginia
June 1988

# 1

**Friday, July 2, 1982**
**Hayward, California**

This date and place mean nothing and everything. Some people claim that they can remember everything about a particular time on a particular date—where they were, what they were doing, what they were wearing—like when Pearl Harbor was bombed or John F. Kennedy was assassinated. I believe it, because the passing of years has not dulled in the least the sharpness of my recollection of the beginning of that Independence Day weekend when events were set into motion that would not only alter my life but which would eventually culminate in a revelation destined to shake the entire nation.

I can run that date like a home movie in forward or reverse, hitting "pause" anytime I want to bring into sharp focus some particular mental image. Everything that transpired on that day is sealed in the inner compartments of my memory and is relived time and time again.

The beat of the music pulsating from the radio did little to quell the growing uneasiness that gnawed at me during the brief drive home from work. I had stayed at my desk during the lunch hour so I could leave early and then enjoy a leisurely shower and a rare nap before going after Christopher. Ignoring the blare of the music, I reviewed the events of the past hours in an attempt to pinpoint the cause of my apprehension. It wasn't difficult at all. The key was Mark's solicitous, almost kind, behavior, so completely foreign to his usual attitude, which regarded me as something he needed to scrape off his shoes.

Mark had followed me to California late in 1981, saying that he wanted to be near Chris, now two years old and the only positive feature of a marriage cursed from its beginning. Mainly for our child's sake, we tried to salvage something of what must have been there in the beginning,

17

but the attempt was fruitless. In May I had moved into
another apartment with Chris, allowing Mark to live in my
former apartment, foolishly leaving the lease and utilities in
my name.

Because of severe problems related to drinking and drugs,
Mark was usually without money and was constantly looking
to me to bail him out of financial difficulties. I was
dumbfounded when he called on Thursday to tell me he
would see me at work the next day to repay some money
he owed me. Mark never repaid a debt with anything
other than insults, and he certainly never took seriously
any obligations to me. My need for money overrode my
instinctive suspicions that were aroused by normal contact
with Mark.

True to his word, Mark arrived at my office at noon the
next day and counted out $60. Then he asked if he could
have Chris for the rest of the day, being responsible for
both his lunch and dinner. A cautionary stab of doubt
about Mark's sincerity made me pause for a moment before
responding. I looked at him, studying his features for the
betrayal of covert intentions. Outwardly there was nothing
but the plea of a father making a reasonable request to be
allowed to spend some time with his son. Still my alarm
mechanism was triggered by the memory of Mark's threats
to take Chris to Maryland. Those threats were usually
lambasted in the midst of a shouting match when Mark was
emboldened by alcohol or marijuana, but I had taken them
seriously enough to give my babysitter strict instructions
that absolutely no one, especially my husband, was to pick
up Chris without my consent.

Perhaps if I hadn't been so tired I might have refused
Mark's request. He began to lift his hand as if in supplication,
but before he could speak I reached for the telephone. "I'll
call Kitty," was all I said. An audible sigh of relief indicated
the tension that escaped Mark. While I was dialing he walked
to the window and looked out at the construction site across
from the building in which I worked. As I chatted with Kitty,

explaining that Mark would come for Chris and listening to her description of one of my child's cute antics, Mark began to pace the floor. Again he looked out the window, his back toward me.

I hung up the phone, but he remained in the same position, as if in deep thought, a mood completely foreign to him. I waited, puzzled by the aura of melancholy that seemed to emanate from him. We had long ago ceased feeling comfortable in each other's presence, and being together for any length of time usually resulted in harsh words. Yet he was apparently reluctant to leave. I noticed a slight sag of his shoulders as he finally turned and faced me. In an apologetic tone that made me want to believe him, he said, "I'm sorry that things didn't work out between us." He had never apologized for anything before and for the moment I was touched. "Me too," I responded. He left after arranging for me to come for Chris early in the evening.

The afternoon passed swiftly as office duties dispelled the nagging feeling that something was wrong. There was nothing specific during Mark's visit that couldn't be explained, but the whole scenario just wasn't Mark. Now that I had opportunity to reflect on our conversation during my drive home, my apprehension began to mount. I deliberately pushed aside the impulse to head straight to Mark's apartment, dismissing my anxiety as natural motherly concern.

It was in the close confines of my shower stall that the panic unexpectedly, inexplicably gripped me. All of a sudden I knew that the worst had happened and that I had to act quickly. Draping myself in a towel, I ran to the telephone. I used all my will power to force my fingers to stop trembling enough to dial Susan's number. Mark had no telephone in his apartment and often used his neighbor's phone.

I managed to calm my voice to nearly normal as I asked Susan if she would mind asking Mark to come to the phone. The delay was almost unbearable while all kinds of muddled imaginings were racing in my mind. Finally came Susan's

breathless report that even though Mark's car was in front of
his apartment, there was no response to her knocking. I asked
her to check with other neighbors, particularly with Chuck,
who frequently joined Mark in doing drugs. Again there was
a lifetime of waiting compressed into the few minutes before
Susan returned to report no knowledge of Mark and Chris.

All my attempts to construct a logical explanation for
the day's events failed to quiet my screaming nerves.
While reason argued that Mark and Chris often walked to
the neighborhood playground or corner grocery, intuitive
certainty countered that their absence was far more serious
than that. Somehow I succeeded in stilling my shaking body
long enough to dress, all the while holding back a cold fear
that threatened to possess me, effectively preventing any
rational course of action.

I had no plan and thought no further than just getting to
Chris. I don't know how I arrived safely at Mark's apartment.
Blinded by tears of fear and fury, I paid respect neither to
traffic signs nor to speed limits. I fully expected my worst
fears to be confirmed but still prayed that I was mistaken. I
couldn't imagine being deprived of my beautiful son—he was
my joy and very reason for living.

Less than an hour had passed from the time I left work
until I braked to an abrupt stop in front of Mark's apartment.
Ordinarily I would not have picked Chris up for another two
hours, but this was more than an ordinary outing of a father
with his little boy. Without bothering to close the car door I
raced to the apartment and rapped on the door. Even though
I knew there would be no answer, I repeatedly knocked, as if
the frantic urgency of my pleas would command a response.
When I finally paused to give my aching knuckles a reprieve,
the silence seemed even more intense.

I looked in the window, straining to peer between the
curtains. Nothing appeared to be amiss, and once again
reason strove to break through my frozen panic, suggesting
that if I only waited a little while I would soon hear
Chris's excited laughter as he and his father returned from

a neighborhood stroll. I clung to that thought for only a moment as I leaned against the window, trying with all my might to will it into reality. It was no use. The very stillness of the scene seemed to confirm my fears.

David! He would surely know something. Residents of the adjacent apartment, David and Liz had been my best friends during the year that I had lived here, and we were still very close. Two steps brought me to their door, which opened immediately upon my first knock. David, I was certain, had been standing there the whole time, probably since I drove up.

He opened the door only a crack, extending no greeting at all. An icy chill engulfed me as I discerned that he had a part to play in this madness. He avoided my eyes as he handed me a set of keys. "Mark said to give you these," was all he said and quickly closed the door. There was no further explanation. The cold reality that I was receiving from a close friend the callous indifference that one would give to a stranger had a brutal effect on me. If there was no sympathetic support here, where was it to be found?

Trusting the loyalty of friendship, I had to get some answers from David. Swallowing the anger surging within me, I again tapped a pleading knock on the door and again it was opened. Where are Mark and Chris? How long have they been gone? Did Mark say when they would return? Is there a message for me? Each question was punctuated by the inflected tones of begging, and to all of them there was only one answer: "Mark said he'll call you later tonight." The door closed in my face as I stood riveted there, my mouth and throat constricted with dryness.

The panic that had crescendoed in dreadful wave after dreadful wave suddenly departed, leaving in its wake an empty numbness, a dullness as profound in its nothingness as the fear had been in its manifestations of terror. I staggered, almost fainting, from the sudden void that consumed me, draining whatever reserve of strength I had. Then I found myself inside Mark's apartment, acting automatically and not remembering unlocking the door.

I hurried through each room, hoping to find some clue to help me understand what was happening. I found it on a small table next to the easy chair in the living room—a piece of scrap paper torn from an envelope on which I saw Mark's pinched handwriting. I read it in a daze, trying to make sense out of it. Mostly it was a jumble of words that defied logic, even had I been in a proper state of mind. Two things, however, stood out clearly—he was taking Chris and he was leaving bills for me to pay. Both the apartment and the utilities were still in my name, and Mark had paid neither rent nor electricity. I was to find later that there was much more.

For some reason I stood vacantly in the middle of the room, scanning its contents. Every piece of furniture in the apartment was mine, left behind for Mark's use when Chris and I moved out. My eyes fell on a large, deep hole burned into the couch by a cigarette when Mark had passed out during a solitary drinking session. The sight of that ugliness caused me to whisper, "He's neither capable nor worthy of taking care of a child."

I took a last look around. I had built a home for Chris here and had struggled with only my own resources to provide the very best for him. Now my baby was stolen from me. Had I known that morning when I kissed him good-bye that it would be three years before I would see him again, I would have lingered a little longer, and held him tighter, and told him in some unforgettable way that a child could lock in his memory just how much I loved him.

Slowly I made my way home, resisting the urge to drive to the bus station, the airport, or anywhere else Mark may have gone to secure transportation out of the city. It was too late. He had planned carefully. What could I do? The police wouldn't help. There was no legal separation, no granting of legal custody, so there was no kidnapping. An expensive attorney was out of the question. I had no money at all, and now Mark's bills were added to my own financial obligations.

I had run the gamut of emotional upheaval in only a few hours. An uneasy suspicion had evolved into a tugging anxiety which soon grew into a monstrous terror with all its attendant expressions. That feeling had subsided into the grief of a throbbing numbness, and now there was only the frustration of utter helplessness and the despair of abject hopelessness. I knew of no one person on the planet to whom I could turn for solace, much less positive direction. There was no caring father or mother to embrace me and rally to my cause, and I could not think of one friend whom I could call upon. I was twenty-two years old, miserably alone in a city of strangers, with a weight far too heavy to carry by myself.

It was in that moment of bleak reflection that the stark realization hit me that whatever help I received would come from no earthly source. Had I foreseen the years of agonizing turmoil that lay before me to test the fiber of my meager faith, my resolve to trust in a God whom I had vaguely known since childhood would have been swept away like chaff in the wind. For the moment, however, there was the faint stirring of microscopic hope.

# 2

## Mid November 1977
## Skowhegan, Maine

The cheer of the evergreens flecked with scattered snowflakes struggled in vain to dispel the dullness that gripped the somber countryside surrounding Skowhegan, Maine. Sadly dismissed were the glorious hues of an autumn that only New England can display. The unvarying drabness gave visible evidence to the mood of my contemplation as I scrutinized one last time the document before me.

After hours of tedious interviews, aptitude tests, medical exams, and security checks, only the signatures of me and my mother needed to be added. Although I believed that our autographs would provide for me an escape from a detestable existence that was becoming more unbearable each day, I felt no particular elation. I simply accepted the realization that my life would be drastically altered in just a few months and that there could be no change of mind. With no intent of being melodramatic, I began to review the circumstances that brought me to this point, particularly those of the last few months.

From the age of eleven I had harbored an intense resolve to leave home by the time I reached eighteen. That commitment had been steeled over the years until it had become an obsession with me. The most contributing factor to my longing to be independent was the tense atmosphere in which I was forced to live. Any semblance of normal family life was rendered impossible by the long absences of my father when he was on patrol with the navy and the ceaseless bickering between him and my mother when he was home. If we children did not hear the sounds of a nightly shouting match emanating from my father's private den below our bedrooms, we knew that either he was on a date or my mother had drunk herself into a stupor.

Dad blamed Mom's alcoholism for all the trouble; Mom

attributed her excessive drinking to Dad's unfaithfulness. It
was a no-win situation, with neither parent willing to accept
blame or compromise. At that time, of course, I was unaware
of my father's espionage activities and the impact they might
have had on his marriage.

After years of constant and bitter tension, the deterioration
of my parent's relationship culminated with my father's
stormy departure one night early in 1975. I lay on my bed
in my upstairs bedroom in the big house on Old Ocean
View Road in Norfolk, Virginia, listening to the thunderous
reverberations of the front door angrily slamming each time
my father removed some of his belongings from the house to
the car.

My concern for what the neighbors might think was
subdued by fears for myself and my older sisters and
younger brother. I tried my hardest to cry. I desperately
wanted to cry, to vent long suppressed feelings. It seemed
to me that a daughter should cry when her Daddy left her,
but no tears came—not even when my father fled without
bothering to explain to us or even to say good-bye. It never
occurred to me that I should try to intervene somehow—to
mediate, beg, or offer hope for reconciliation. The break in
our family was hopelessly irrevocable, and I had expected
this hour for a long time.

I wasn't really surprised that Dad didn't pause to
acknowledge his children, even if I did keep listening for
his step on the stairs. I had no reason to expect him to act
otherwise, considering his past performance. I was not quite
fifteen years old and could not remember the last time my
father praised me, cuddled me, playfully teased me, or spoke
an endearing word to me. He customarily referred to my
sisters, my mother, and me as "the bitches." In fact, when he
moved out he told only my brother Michael where he was
living and instructed him not to let "the bitches" know where
he was.

Notwithstanding the fact that the tension in our house
would probably be alleviated considerably, the manner of

my father's departure still hurt dreadfully. The rejection that I had sensed from my early childhood had already caused me to do deplorable things, and now it seemed to have been completed. The disregard that my father exhibited toward us was exemplified by an incident that took place a few months after he left us.

My sister Cynthia and I entered a Norfolk seafood restaurant with our boyfriends when we saw Dad at a table with a woman. He looked up and met our eyes with an icy glare that warned us not to approach his table. Then he turned, picked up his drink and continued his conversation. There was no hint of recognition, not even a nod, much less a smile.

To this day memories of my father's denials of me hurt grievously. Over the years I have wondered what he was thinking when he saw my sister and me in the restaurant. Was there sorrow? Remorse? Relief from the burden of parental responsibility? We were his children. How could he refuse to acknowledge us? I never did discuss my pain with him, nor question him about his feelings. Perhaps I should have . . .

Outwardly, my father's departure from the household had little effect on my mother. She had been existing in a dreary vacuum for several years with her alcoholism out of control and with no desire for deliverance. Sometimes she would sit for hours drinking alone in the darkness of the family room in the big five-bedroom house. We would hear nothing except the sound of her crying until she drank herself to sleep.

It was frightful for us to see her in such a condition, but not a one of us children knew what to do or say. We knew nothing about comforting others, since we received none ourselves, and had only been taught self-sufficiency. There was no teacher, minister, or close relative in whom we could confide, nor would we had there been. Even when Mom left us alone for several days to go to the hospital for surgery, she gave no explanation. To this day I'm still not certain of the nature of the surgery.

My mother's periods of solitude were actually the best
times for us. At other times her alcoholism had far nastier
manifestations. She would be completely irrational, violent,
and abusive. At such times we stayed away from home as
much as possible to avoid screaming fights. Total evasion
was impossible, however, and there were some ugly
encounters. Laughter would infuriate my mother sooner
than curses shouted in anger, probably because she was
so unhappy herself.

One evening we were recounting the day's activities at
the dinner table, when a remark by Michael evoked laughter
from us girls. When Mom's voluble protests served only to
quiet the jovial clamor to a slightly subdued round of titters,
she stood to her feet, picked up the table and turned it over,
dumping its contents in the laps of the diners. Needless to
say, we saturated the room with our absence.

Perhaps if I had been endowed with the mercy that looks
beyond circumstances to contributory causes, I could have
understood my mother's self-effacing behavior and perhaps
attempt to minister some degree of healing. As it was, I
knew nothing of the nightmarish existence provoked by
Dad's double life. Nor did I consider her poverty-stricken
and odious background.

She was from a family of seven children and lost her father,
whom she adored, when he suddenly collapsed while the two
of them were walking along a beach. She was only nine years
old. Her mother was both selfish and promiscuous, the type
who would eat a banana split while her children had nothing
at all. She brought home a succession of lovers, and it was not
uncommon for my mother and the others to witness sex acts.

This conduct carried over to the children. Mom shared
a bed with an older sister who was just as trashy as their
mother. Sometimes Mom would wake up as her sister was
having sex in the same bed with a man she had picked up.
There was also incest as well as other forms of abuse.

Instead of extending the grace of compassionate tolerance
with regard to my mother's condition, my siblings and I

indulged ourselves in unrestrained rebellion. With no
paternal guidance or supervision and no role models other
than the rock stars whose concerts I religiously attended, my
life settled into a pattern of ruinous debasement. I had just
turned fifteen, and after being hooked on cigarettes for
three years, I turned to marijuana, which was always easily
obtainable.

Cynthia and I skipped school whenever we felt like it,
hanging around pool halls all day. Many times I didn't
bother to go home at all, staying with friends or sleeping
outside. Starved for affection, I chose a poor substitute by
yielding to a promiscuous lifestyle.

My ungoverned activities soon got me in trouble with
the authorities, and I spent two weeks in a juvenile detention
center awaiting a court appearance. The only things that
impressed me about my period of confinement were my
mother's failure to visit me, showing absolutely no concern,
and the fact that only detainees sixteen and older could
smoke, depriving me of what I regarded as a stern necessity.
My court hearing resulted in a rigid one-year probation.

Paradoxically, it was during this time that I had my first
serious encounter with spiritual matters. The only person on
both sides of my family who could be called religious was my
fraternal grandmother, who practiced a brand of Catholicism
mixed with occult activities, such as tarot card reading. My
mother did not believe in any kind of redemption. There was
only God sitting on a throne overseeing things and apparently
doing a poor job of it. The only prayers I was ever taught
were the "Our Father" and the "Hail Mary."

I was both stunned and mystified when Margaret, my sister
who was two years older than me, informed me that she had
been "saved" at the local Baptist church. I didn't know what
she was talking about but accompanied her to the church.
Soon I was crying my way through a prayer for salvation.
For several weeks I was faithful in attending church, but
no one took time to disciple me, and I certainly received no
encouragement from home. I never read the Bible and didn't

know that I should. Like the seed in the Lord's parable that
fell on the beaten path, whatever had been planted in me
was soon snatched away. As I was to discover much later,
God's unconquerable grace was at work even then.

The depressing situation at home was rapidly becoming
more hopeless as fights between my mother and me occurred
more frequently, evolving from shouting matches to more
violent confrontations. My life was a mess, and I placed all
the blame for it on a totally irresponsible mother. In turn, she
found it impossible to deal with my incorrigible behavior. I
was sliding downhill on greased skids and there appeared to
be nothing to brake my descent.

The total collapse of our relationship happened not long
after my sixteenth birthday. Mom's objection to what she
considered to be my rakish appearance touched off the fuse
to a bomb of pent-up furies waiting to explode. The scene
that followed both inside and outside the house was no mere
domestic squabble, albeit tempestuous. The ugly eruption of
seething emotions that had been brewing for months in each
of us spewed forth a torrent of anathematic words that no
mother and daughter should even entertain toward each
other, much less rend the public air with them. She actually
challenged me to a scratching, hair-pulling, no-holds-barred
fight on the front lawn, and only my superior size and
strength kept us from a physical altercation.

Instead, we stared each other down, neither one admitting
victory or defeat. Finally, with a tone of finality and
resignation, Mom tersely informed me that she had all she
could take from me and that she was sending me to Maine to
stay with her sister's family in their rambling farmhouse, at
least for the summer. Nothing she could have said would have
made me more agreeable. After all, I had run away from
home many times, and now I was being given the opportunity
to leave without sneaking off.

I had only met Aunt Annie and two of her seven children
briefly a few months earlier when they came to Norfolk for
a short visit. Now I met Uncle Bob and my other cousins as

I moved in with them on their large acreage near Anson, Maine. I fit right in, especially since one of their largest crops was marijuana. Several of the kids smoked pot, and the parents never objected. I thought it strange, then, that Uncle Bob didn't approve of cigarettes. I could smoke homegrown Mary Jane in front of him but not store-bought Philip Morris.

I got along well with the family, especially Cindy, who was the same age as my sister Cynthia. We both had the same interests—pool, boys, and pot—and we indulged all three. I was definitely on a trip and was riding in the driver's seat with the pedal to the floor in the express lane of a clear road. It was summertime for sure.

Then my euphoric balloon was pricked by a formidable announcement from my mother. My stay in Maine was not to be temporary but permanent. That part of the news wasn't so disappointing, but the rest of it was devastating. By this time, my parents' divorce was final, so Mom had decided to move herself and the other children into the farmhouse with us. My steamy reaction on the telephone communicated quite sufficiently the instantaneous rage that burned white hot within me. I had just escaped the bedlam of life with my mother, and now it was following me, and would be compounded by the hubbub of twelve people under one roof. Under the best of circumstances, no house was big enough for the brawling mother-daughter pair that we were, so I couldn't imagine how we could tolerate each other in the midst of ten other people.

Once my family arrived, however, the situation was altogether different from what my fears expected. In retrospect, I can attribute it to the fact that we were brought together out of necessity to face a common adversity. We were quartered in attic rooms which we had to clean, and I began to notice certain features about the household that had escaped me before. Margaret, who was vociferous in declaring her hatred of the place, first called my attention to the squalid filth that had accumulated in every room. I suppose my pot-clouded eyes hadn't been able to detect such things, and the pungent odor of marijuana smoke wafting about the place overcame all other smells. Margaret nevertheless was right. Untidy is too pretty a word to describe the house. It was a pigsty, with no offense intended the pigs.

My relatives' habits of personal hygiene wouldn't exactly bring home blue ribbons from a health fair. It was 1976, and these people were still bathing in the same water, that is, when they decided to bathe. In the five months we were there neither Uncle Bob nor his sons bathed once, and Aunt Annie took one shower. To take care of our own needs, my mother bought a portable shower, but we were allowed to take only one shower a week.

Uncle Bob kept a movie projector set up beside his bed on which he ran pornographic movies. On the floor beside the bed were hundred of wads of used tissues. The disgusting scene was nauseous even to me, and I was definitely no virginal Gidget.

Tension mounted rapidly in the overloaded household. The Walkers detested the lazy country folks for their unpardonable sloppiness, and the Nelsons resented the intrusive city folks for eating their food, notwithstanding the fact that my mother bought the provisions. At the time I didn't understand why Mom gave up a comfortable house in Norfolk to come to this mess.

The breaking point came one day when all the Nelson family were gone, except for Jennifer, the youngest daughter. Some of Mom's clothes had been disappearing, and I was convinced that my cousin Cindy had taken them since she was the only one who could wear that size. I was determined to find the missing items. With Michael's help I began to search the house. We found them stashed away in her parents' bedroom. Unfortunately, Jennifer saw us taking the clothes and began to hurl all kinds of poisonous verbal darts at us. When she persisted, Michael simply slugged her.

Jennifer may have been clamped down, but now we had the rest of the family to contend with. Cindy and I were the

next combatants, and I'm convinced that in my punitive rage
I would have scarred her for life had I not been restrained.
Order was restored only when Mom announced that we were
leaving.

Margaret went to Boston to stay with relatives while the
rest of us moved into a tiny house in Skowhegan. I had to
share a cramped room with Michael. For privacy's sake we
tacked a blanket to the ceiling that was reminiscent of the
"wall of Jericho" that stood between Claudette Colbert and
Clark Gable in *It Happened One Night*. Cynthia, who would
soon give birth to a child out of wedlock, had a room to
herself.

It didn't take me long to find a circle of friends with whom
I could continue my established lifestyle. I found a real jewel
in Pammy. There was action at her house every weekend
when her mother was staying with her boyfriend. All of us
would pool our money to buy liquor and pot, gather at
Pammy's house, turn the rock music on full volume, and
proceed to get wasted. Some of the debauchery is better left
undescribed.

I was classified among my peers as a "head," and I did
my worst to deserve the rating. Not a day went by that I
didn't go to school high, and at every break during the day
I withdrew to the smoking area to smoke pot with my
friends. Amazingly, we never got caught.

My closest friend outside of school was a male cousin,
eleven years older than I, who had just gone through a
divorce. We were constant companions, even to the extent
of going on overnight trips together. Although people
suspected a sexual relationship between us, there was never
any substance to the rumors. What most people didn't know
was that he was a drug dealer, and I accompanied him on
distribution trips. He introduced me to cocaine and kept me
supplied with both coke and pot.

Such was my existence as the months passed.
Unfortunately, I dragged Michael down with me. He
was only fourteen years old, but he was as deeply involved

as I in pot and partying. He joined me in getting high every
morning before we left for school. His attitude was outwardly
manifested in his long hair and manner of dress. Although the
school authorities classified him as rebellious, I saw him as a
confused adolescent set on a maddening roller-coaster ride by
our domestic situation. I certainly didn't help stabilize him.

It wasn't long before Michael was expelled from public
school. Mom was forced to find a private tutor for him. To
his credit, Michael accepted the discipline of working on the
tutor's farm in order to cover the tuition. There was a marked
improvement in his attitude, and he was allowed to return to
school the following year. It later proved to be no blessing
when my father offered to take Michael when he turned
sixteen.

We moved from the tiny house on French Street to a
more spacious duplex on Maple Street soon after Cynthia's
baby was born in February 1977. She had dropped out of
school and wasn't interested in finishing by correspondence.
Mom constantly browbeat her and sometimes would even
strike her. The abuse that my mother inflicted on my sister
haunts me to this day.

Financially, we had to stretch our necks considerably
to catch a dim view of the poverty line. Mom's divorce
settlement gave her the title to the house in Norfolk and
two properties out of state. She foolishly left it all, without
receiving any compensation, to come to Maine. My father,
supposing he had an appointment to see Mom, found the
house empty and moved back in. As far as the real estate is
concerned, Mom never paid the taxes, much less tried to
sell it, and it reverted to the civil government. The court
also ordered Dad to pay $200 monthly to each of us, a total
of $1,000. He rarely complied, and his payments were at best
sporadic. They soon ceased altogether.

Mom was stitching shoes, I was slinging hamburgers,
and Michael was shoveling snow, but our combined incomes,
augmented by food stamps, were barely sufficient. I had no
new clothes during my two years of school in Skowhegan

and was often subjected to cruel remarks by insensitive classmates. I had come to Maine from Norfolk during the summer, so my clothes were not fit for the harsh winters. I didn't own a coat, so all winter I wore a sweatshirt underneath one of Michael's jeans jackets. My classmates thought I dressed myself in this nondescript fashion merely to focus attention on myself.

My opportunity to escape was offered in the fall of my senior year. Pammy persuaded me to go with her to our school's career seminar to listen to the military recruiters' spiel, suggesting that it would be great if we could enlist in the Army under the buddy system. The idea was foreign to me, and I wasn't remotely interested. My indifference quickly gave way to attentiveness when I saw that one of the young recruiters was a cute former neighbor from French Street. Not long into the convincing presentation, I became a convert to the salvation they were offering. I was realistic enough to know that Army barracks were not built on Easy Street in Fat City, but Pudgy Town was a vast improvement on my present circumstances.

Most likely, any thought of college was out of the question for me. My history of erratic high school attendance had resulted in terrible grades. There was also no way I could afford it. Nor could I see much of a future behind a hamburger and chicken nugget counter.

Pammy's enthusiasm fizzled after a couple of days, but I grew more excited as I contemplated the advantages the Army would offer me. If anything, my mother was even more enthusiastic and assured me her full support. I don't know if she was more interested in my welfare or in a more peaceful household.

I penned my name with a little more flair than usual to the paper that officially enlisted me in the delayed entry program. Eight months later I would enter active duty, only three months after my eighteenth birthday.

Shortly after enlisting, I learned the devastating status of my progress toward graduation. I would have to spend

another year in school to complete credits that I was lacking.
Since I was already carrying a full academic load, my only
other option was correspondence courses. That avenue,
however, was closed to me because I had no money to pay
for them. Without graduation, there was no Army in my
future.

My rescue came from a totally unexpected source. I had
had no contact with my father during the year and a half
that I had been in Maine. He had effectively cut himself off
from the family and took no initiative to establish any kind of
relationship with his children. Now, however, I felt desperate
enough to follow Mom's advice to seek his help. To my
astonishment, he seemed genuinely concerned when I called
in December to tell him of my predicament.

He expressed gushing praise at my decision to enter the
Army, especially when he learned that I would be trained
as a communications specialist. His encouragement found
tangible expression in an offer to bear the expense of my
correspondence courses. Although the amount wasn't
staggering—no more than $150—it was to me the only real
affection my father had shown me in years. I had no way of
knowing that his renewed interest in me was not prompted by
fatherly concern, but rather by his own selfish designs.

For the remaining six months of the academic year I
sternly applied myself to disciplined study. I really had no
choice if I wanted to complete correspondence courses,
which normally took a year to finish, in addition to my
regular classes. This was the first time in my life that I had
set a goal and persevered in reaching it. Up to this point I
had never considered anything else worth the effort.

Mom was impressed by my diligence, and our relationship
improved, mostly because I had no time to argue. Other
activities, however, suffered little. I was still heavily into
drugs and promiscuity. I even became deeply involved with
a man fifteen years my senior, married but separated from
his wife. I spent every available minute with him until we

were practically living together. Over the strong objections of my mother, and against my awareness that this man never regarded me as anything other than a convenient sexual playmate, I persisted in the relationship.

It would be untrue to say that I was without moral restraint during those years of youthful indulgence; conscience had not altogether deserted me. Whatever spiritual sensitivity had been awakened in me still groaned at my dissolute lifestyle. It may seem ludicrous to speak of God's grace at work in the midst of such wanton activity, but I can only ascribe to that divine attribute the fact that I was spared venereal disease, pregnancy, harsher drug dependency, and a hundred more ills attendant to such a profligate way of living. Not only that, but I was kept from utter abandonment to unbridled debauchery.

In no way can I excuse my coarse behavior, but I do plead a tolerant understanding of the rejection which I had felt for so long. Unfortunately, this scenario is repeated countless times as emotionally battered children, caught up in the maelstrom of domestic warfare, struggle in various ways for the recognition and affection which they have been denied at home. The damage inflicted upon children as a result of parental neglect and abuse, whether verbal or physical, leaves ugly scars that beg for healing. All too often, the wrong balm is applied, serving only to deepen the wounds.

My graduation was rapidly approaching, and I was feeling a justified sense of accomplishment. My elation was chilled, however, by the realization that I would not have an appropriate dress for the commencement ceremonies. The prom was not even a remote possibility. I had to borrow a dress to wear to the graduation dinner. My mother's failure to provide me with clothes fitting for these and other occasions provoked deep-seated resentment in me.

It wasn't just the lack of clothes that was so exasperating, but I was continually outraged by Mom's favoritism toward Margaret. She was always providing my sister with

unaffordable gifts of clothing and jewelry. Mom didn't bother
to attend my graduation, preferring to sit and drink before
the television set.

It was the custom at the graduation dinner for the student
council to present gifts, usually novelty items, appropriate for
each graduate. One girl received a set of chattering teeth in
recognition of her talkative nature, while a boy was given a
toy watch to remind him of his constant tardiness. I was
presented with a new blouse, with the comment that now
I would have some decent clothes to wear. Although things
were done in jest, and not meant to be taken seriously, I
was humiliated. I remember thinking that soon I would be
wearing a smart new uniform.

Two weeks before I was to report to Fort Jackson, South
Carolina, my father flew to Maine in his plane and brought
me back to Norfolk. The kindness and consideration that he
displayed were atypical of his previous attitude toward me.
He gave me a clock radio and some clothes as going-away
gifts, and he also took me out for an evening of dancing. I
wallowed in the attention he gave me, gladdened that I had
finally done something to merit my father's pride.

While it was bewildering to be treated like the daughter of
a doting father, I didn't for a moment entertain the suspicion
that he was setting me up. That stabbing realization came all
too soon.

# 3

August 1978
Fort Gordon, Georgia

Fort Gordon is cursed by thousands of raw recruits who chaff at the rigorous discipline of the military life they have chosen. For me, however, the atmosphere was an invigorating elixir of which I could drink and never be filled. Even though I contributed my groans to the myriad grumblings uttered daily by homesick enlistees, inwardly I luxuriated in being a part of this vast proving ground. The bullheaded independence that I had always asserted in the form of prodigal rebellion was now for the first time harnessed to the accomplishment of something positive. Conversely, there was nothing at home for which I pined.

The eager industry that I invested in meeting the challenges of boot camp brought visible dividends. Very early in the program I was named the senior squad leader of our company, and toward its conclusion I ranked second in the competition to receive the outstanding trainee award. Scholastically I was astounding even myself as I studied to become a radio operator, missing only one test question during the entire course. My achievements were even more fulfilling because I was one of only eight girls in the entire company of eighty trainees.

It was late Saturday night, and I was both tired and exhilarated. My weariness was the result of a tremendously active day, and my stimulation was generated by the charming and laudatory attention my father had lavished on me since his surprise arrival that morning. The reefer that we had just shared in his hotel room contributed to the lift as well.

It had been an eminently satisfying day, and the tired contentment I felt as I entered my barracks was fully justified. I didn't know how, but my father managed to have the run of the base and to arrange a pass for me.

John Walker has a dynamic personality and can be quite winsome and convincing while plotting to achieve his ends. He also knew how to enjoy a party, eliciting boisterous laughter from a crowded room and making certain that he was the center of attention. So our evening of dining and dancing was a fun-filled success. Afterwards we talked for hours at his hotel, with our conversation consisting mostly of my responses to his leading questions.

He was interested in every facet of my training, and searched out even the most insignificant details concerning my familiarity with radio equipment. He wanted to know the nomenclature and purpose of every component, procedure for changing codes, security arrangements, and the like.

On that occasion I saw nothing unusual in his interest, because, after all, he had spent most of his naval career as a communications expert. To me it appeared that he was on a nostalgia trip, or merely comparing his methods with my own training. At any rate, he offered me practical advice and strong encouragement to be doggedly resolute in establishing a good military record. I returned to the base reveling in the thought that my Dad cared enough for me that he would come all the way from Norfolk just to spend the day with me.

My decision to enlist in the Army had not only provided a way of escape from a miserable home life but evidently had elevated me to a position that merited my father's respect. From the moment he learned of my enlistment, a paternal pride and concern that had been dammed up for years suddenly gushed over me. Not once before then had he made an effort to contact me in Maine, much less exercise a father's responsibility in seeing to his daughter's welfare.

I supposed that his reborn interest was motivated by gratification that one of his children had chosen to pattern a career after his own. Given Dad's past behavior, and knowing him as I did, I should have suspected that he never exerted any effort except to achieve a selfish intent. Kindness and generosity were not among his most notable virtues. At the time, my only thought concerning my father's actions, so incongruous with his previous dealings with me, was that I had finally done something to please him and thus merit the sudden attention that he was uncharacteristically lavishing upon me.

I had spent two weeks with Dad in Norfolk after he brought me from Maine in his private plane. I had not been in the city for two years, and Dad financed shopping sprees and entertainment excursions for me and my friends. He showed me off around his circle of acquaintances, bragging on me to the hilt.

The climax to this hectic pre-induction activity was the going away party that Dad staged for my benefit. He played to perfection the role of an affectionate father bursting with pride. The speech that he made to the guests was flavored with patriotic fervor as he recalled his own military career. The capstone came when he ceremoniously presented me with his officer's saber so I could cut the cake.

That evening confirmed to me more than anything else the soundness of my decision to enter the Army. Something that could work such a change in my father's attitude toward me could be nothing else than the proper course of action.

The next day Dad talked incessantly as he drove me to the bus station, mostly giving me advice on how to get along with the system and impress my superiors. Anyone witnessing our farewell would have been moved by the display of a father's emotion as he bade good-bye to his brave teen-age daughter going away to face a hostile world all alone.

To tell the truth, I was sincerely touched myself as Dad hugged me, manifesting an affection he had not revealed in years. I made myself believe that there was even the hint of tears in his eyes and a catch in his voice. His parting word to me was a solemn promise that he would write often.

I took his vow lightly because I had never received a personal letter from him. Surprisingly, he kept his word, and letters soon began to arrive regularly. Dad wrote just as he talked, and his letters were always light and breezy, spiced

with a mixture of humor and profanity. He invariably
bolstered my self-image with expressions of his pride in me
and offered me advice on how to get ahead, encouraging
me to exert all my energies to excel in every phase of my
training.

One letter in particular has stayed fresh in my memory
because its receipt provided me with the kind of selfish
security that one of several children feels when her father
assures her that he is sharing an intimate secret only with
her. Dad wrote that even though he tried not to show it (his
restraint had been remarkably successful), I was his favorite
child, and he had always known that I would be the one who
would make him the proudest by my accomplishments.

Assurances like that can be heady to a child who for years
had received only intermittent doses of her father's attention
and was now suddenly engulfed in it. I drank it greedily, as a
wino takes to a bottle after a long dry spell. I wanted to
please my father, so I plunged myself into my training
program with a gritty determination to win his approval.

As I lay on my bed in my Spartan quarters, too tired and
excited to sleep, I reflected on my family's past in light of the
present situation and tried to remember when things began to
fall apart. I had never experienced the stability of being
anchored firmly to the immovable foundation built by the
assurance of being wanted.

That my parents loved each other was obvious, and
four children were born to them before they were
twenty-five-years old. I was the third child, born two and
a half years after Margaret and only eleven months after
Cynthia. No child should have to grow up burdened by the
knowledge that he or she was both unplanned and
unwelcome—as my mother informed me. Cynthia was a
sickly baby, and Mom hated the thought of being pregnant
while caring for her, not to mention the hardship of having a
trio of babies under the age of three.

Dad was furious at the news of Mom's pregnancy,

complaining that he could not support the family on his
meager pay as a low-ranking sailor. Mom described to me
how she often tried to cause a miscarriage by exerting herself
to the limit with heavy work and even by deliberately falling
downstairs.

My father, reconciled to having another child, hoped that
it would at least be a boy. Upon learning from a nurse that
he was the father of another girl, he stormed out of the
hospital without bothering to see either me or my mother.
"Tell my wife I'll see her later," he muttered to the nurse.
"Later" turned out to be three days.

When I was old enough to understand, both parents
assured me of their love for me and demonstrated it in many
ways during my childhood, but that in itself could never
completely overcome the insecurity caused by what they told
me concerning my birth.

Michael's arrival marked a distinct change in the
atmosphere of our home. He was irresistible, and Dad
became the typical doting father. The next few years were
the best of my life as Dad devoted himself to the family.
He was a fun person and could entertain us for hours with
various antics and sportive activities. He was highly
imaginative, able to transform the simplest event into an
adventurous undertaking. A trip to the beach would be a trek
across the Sahara, a hike in the woods was actually a big
game safari in the jungles of darkest Africa or an exploration
of frontier America led by Daniel Boone.

Nothing was commonplace to him; everything was a game
to be played or a drama to be enacted. Even holidays were
staged events, complete with scripts and movie camera.
Naturally my inventive father was the writer, director, and
cameraman. Every member of the family had a role to
perform, and each tried to upstage the other. Dad's lively
creativity was a delight to us all and kept the whole family in
a state of suspense and expectancy concerning what the next
adventure would be.

Days when he was home were varied, with museum trips,

sightseeing excursions, picnics, movies, and similar activities. To the children he was a fascinating figure who seemed to know everything about anything. He was even an excellent cook, and often the aroma of tempting, sinful goodies permeated the house. During this time we dutifully occupied a pew in the local Catholic church practically every Sunday.

All in all, the John Walker family of the mid sixties was a beamingly happy unit, cemented by harmonious togetherness. Foreboding cracks, however, soon appeared in the foundations of the household, threatening to topple the superstructure.

The first signs that I can recall of tension between my parents were in 1967, when we moved to Ladson, South Carolina. To augment his income from the Navy, my father decided to open a combination restaurant/bar. He secured a building, remodeled it with an oriental theme—lots of bamboo and beaded curtains to lend an exotic look—and furnished it with a bar, tables and chairs, pinball machines, and a pool table. It was appropriately dubbed The Bamboo Snack Bar. We lived in a mobile home behind the establishment.

The Bamboo wasn't an instant success. Not even my father's garrulous salesmanship and resourceful propagandizing could escalate the volume of business. Oh, he tried!

One of his more imaginative attempts aimed to reach the college crowd at a nearby Baptist college, conveying to them an image of the delights of an evening at the cozy Bamboo, rivaling those of the best night spots of Charleston.

I suppose he failed to consider the type of students he was trying to entice because he had fliers printed in which one of the regular cartoon characters from *Playboy* magazine fleshed out the attractions at the new hangout. The verb is appropriate in light of the fact that the cartoon character happened to be a busty siren wearing only a beguiling smile and intriguing thigh-high black leather boots. I remember her well, because I folded and placed one of the fliers under the windshield wipers of every car parked on the college campus. I also remember that, while there was no noticeable increase in business, nobody discarded the advertisements. I thought it was decent of the students not to litter.

Dad attributed the small response to the fact that he was unable to obtain a liquor license. I couldn't understand that explanation, since alcoholic drinks were always available at the Bamboo from bountiful supplies stashed in the closets of our trailer.

It was during this time that my parents began to fight regularly. Brawling parents never seem to consider the effect that their constant squabbles have on their children, especially when adult frustrations are vented on young minds, bodies, and emotions. The atmosphere in our trailer was charged with tension, and we children often huddled together while our parents spent their rage on each other, fearful that one or both of them would light into us next.

Dad ceased to be a fun person, at least with us, if not with customers at the snack bar. He had neither time nor inclination to play games with us, but rather was pulled away from us by some competitive force against which we were powerless. More and more he seemed to absolve himself of all responsibility toward his family.

With a crowd, he was still the same swaggering merrymaker. With me and my siblings, he had become a sharp-tongued, ill-tempered crab who would win hands down any election for prime minister of depression. Many nights we lay listening to the sounds of sportive bacchanalia vibrating from next door, all the while aching for our father to laugh with us, to keep us secure in his presence, and to whisper a soft "good night."

I suppose that childish reflections can exaggerate a situation, but the change in my father's behavior was so meteoric and severe that the stinging slap of rejection that pained the senses of a seven year old can still be keenly felt. My father's abdication of his rights and responsibilities as a parent signaled the beginning of a dismal journey that totally disrupted our family structure and destroyed individual lives.

My mother's participation in this ugly deterioration of family sanctity was no less damnable. By nature she was already emotionally high-strung, but now she had become hazardously explosive. Compounding the problem was the fact that it was during this time that she began to drink more seriously. If violence is more damaging than negligence, then we children suffered more under our mother than under our father. Her anger found expression in both verbal and physical assaults.

One episode stands out above all others as an example of the trauma that I suffered as a result of Mom's actions. She was attempting without success to teach me how to tell time. The more frustrated she got, the louder she screamed, demanding that I tell her the correct time. When I couldn't, she set upon me with a brutal beating in which she slapped me unrelentingly. The emotional injury inflicted upon me was so suppressive that it was not until the fourth grade that I learned to read a clock.

In the midst of this abuse I began to have frightening nightmares at frequent intervals. Many times I would awaken during the night paralyzed at the sight of weird phenomena in my room. Once I saw birds flying from behind a mirror. On another occasion I saw an enormous snake emerge from a wall and slither across the floor. These and similar occurrences left an indelible impression upon me.

The fearful insecurity of my home life manifested itself in other ways. Terrified at what my mother's reaction would be when she saw them, I hid my school papers from her. My grades were excellent, but a sense of inadequacy caused me to shudder at the thought of punishment for not doing better.

A worse pattern developed when I began stealing candy and other small items from the local general store. I never got caught and thus became entrenched in a furtive habit that held me in its grip for several years.

I do not claim inculpability for my actions, but at the same

time I do understand the contributing factors that rejection
and instability were in my upbringing. I read that children
can sense being rejected and unloved even in the womb. It
must be true because those feelings had been my albatross for
the duration of my young life and now were bearing bitter
fruit. Unfortunately, I knew no real deliverance and sought
escape through any promising door. The results were tragic.

We moved to Norfolk in 1968. There were no preliminaries
to prepare us for the transition. Our parents were not ones to
call a family conference to discuss matters that affected us.
We children were simply loaded into the car and driven to
Virginia. Dad had already been living there for months, but
we were not even informed of that. The first we knew of the
change of residence was when we parked in front of a large
apartment building and were told that this was where we
would be living.

Even apart from comparison to our little indigent trailer,
there was no question that the Algonquin House was a classy
establishment. We were trading imitation baloney for T-bone
steak. The whole place reeked of elegance, from the graceful
facade and Chesterfieldian doorman outside to the ornate
lobby and cultivated receptionist inside. There was also
plenty to beckon youthful explorers, such as conference
rooms, recreation rooms, and a beauty salon. There was more
in the rear. An Olympic-size swimming pool enticed us from
the beginning, as well as a lake for boating and fishing.

We may have been profoundly impressed when we
entered the building, but we were flabbergasted upon
viewing our second-floor apartment. The opulence of
the place overwhelmed us. Every piece of furniture was
exquisitely new, consisting of costly teakwood tables, a
hand-embroidered couch, the finest bedroom suites, and
chairs of teakwood, leather, and velvet. Delicate china filled
a huge buffet, and a sophisticated bar was well stocked with
expensive liquor. Beautiful statues and dainty figurines
complimented desks, dressers, and tables. Never before had
I been in the midst of such magnificence.

That night, as my sisters and I excitedly discussed the
abrupt change in our style of living, we decided that one of
several things had happened: a rich relative died, the Bamboo
was a more prosperous business than it outwardly appeared to
be, the Navy paid better in Virginia than in South Carolina,
or Dad had taken a second job. How little we knew.

The quarrels between my parents escalated in frequency,
openness, and tumultuousness. Now there were more visible
signs of their fights as my father became increasingly abusive
toward my mother. We children would often hear the sounds
of his blows midst angry cries and shouted insults as we
cloistered ourselves in a bedroom and vainly tried to support
one another. It was not uncommon for Mom to exhibit two
black eyes for weeks at a time. During these brawls expensive
furniture and other articles would often suffer damage.

Mom herself was becoming more violent, but her savagery
was usually directed toward the children, especially Cynthia.
She had always manifested a brutish nature in her
relationship with my sister, but now her actions were
dangerously past cruelty.

Mom's volcanic and irrational behavior often included
scenes in which she choked Cynthia, sometimes to the point
of unconsciousness. Time and again, the rest of us would have
to intervene on behalf of our defenseless sister. The first such
occasion I can remember was when Cynthia was only eight
years old, and it was repeated until she was into her twenties.
Once Michael was alone in his room when a premonitory urge
drove him to check Cynthia's room. There he found our
drunken mother astride her inert body, strangling the life
from her. Both Michael and Cynthia were convinced that only
his timely intrusion saved her. No physical abuse such as was
inflicted upon Cynthia is ever deserved, but in her case the
tragedy was intensified by the fact that she had done
absolutely nothing to incur Mom's wrath. Of all the children,
she was the most respectful to our parents.

I was only nine years old, but old enough to realize the
relentless deterioration that transformed our happy and

secure household into a pressurized cauldron constantly
gurgling with poisonous malevolence. The pot had boiled over
regularly during the two years that it had been on the heat.
We were strangers to one another. Family affairs were
conducted in a perfunctory manner. Perhaps the worst part of
our plight was the fact that we children were made to bear
the guilt of our parent's disintegrating relationship, and it was
quite clear to us that dispensing parental care was a
distasteful chore to them rather than an enjoyable privilege.

I was growing up in the belief that love was painful. Even
in those tranquil moments when our parents were at peace
with one another and with us, allowing the family an
interlude of normal and enjoyable activity, no warmth was
communicated. My logic was formulated in infantile
simplicity: parents love their children . . . I was receiving
"love" from my parents . . . therefore, love hurts.

That dispassionate reasoning was reinforced by my school
experiences in Norfolk. Dad had enrolled us in a small
private school operated by an austere couple who exercised
discipline by the board of education. That board, which to
my bulging eyes looked to be at least six feet long and a foot
wide, was well worn. Innocent and guilty alike felt the sting
of its resounding whack at least on a weekly basis. In
Michael's case, however, it was a daily ritual. The wielder
of the dreaded instrument always prefaced the corporal
punishment with a blighty "I love you." Is it any wonder that
I was justified in believing that those who love will not
hesitate to hurt?

After a year in Norfolk we moved to San Diego, where we
continued to experience affluence. My father bought a huge
fashionable house that spelled luxury in upper-case letters.
The only negative feature was the landscaping, or rather the
lack of it. All the lawns in the neighborhood were beautifully
coiffured in the latest style with verdant ivy that grew
profusely everywhere but in our front yard. Dad worked us in
the yard for hours in an effort to speed its growth, but
neither our toil nor his curses had any effect on the isolated

little sprigs that stubbornly refused to congregate themselves
in an exuberant entwinement. I still maintain a fervent
hostility toward the plant.

It soon became apparent that my father regarded his family
as an impediment to his self-improvement program. A man
saddled unfairly with the burden of a wife and four children
isn't able to pursue the kind of lifestyle that he desired. The
solution was devilishly simple. If an obstacle is in the way,
walk around it, which is exactly what Dad did with us. He
became like a carefree bachelor, enjoying the good life, while
for the most part we were unceremoniously ignored.

My father's new passions included flying and sailing, and
he became exceptionally adept at both. He soon acquired a
pilot's license and spent hours fulfilling the fantasies of a
pretentious daredevil. His new twenty-four-foot, limited
edition Dolphin sailboat, however, brought him the most
satisfaction, if for no other reason than for the fact that it
won him the greater acclaim. The boat also gave him ample
opportunity to fulfill fantasies of another kind, as he and his
new buddy, Jerry Whitworth, entertained local ladies while
plowing the waves between San Diego and Ensenada.
Sometimes they would be gone for days at a time.

Dad was always an accomplished hot-air artist, and he was
successful in gaining membership in the prestigious and
exclusive San Diego Yacht Club. He spent a great deal of
time at the clubhouse playing the big shot. His infidelity was
becoming outrageously brazen and shamefully humiliating to
Mom. As a result, her drinking problem became worse and
her abuse of us more severe.

My father's verbal harassment of the children had evolved
into actual physical maltreatment. For the past three years
he had been harshly demanding and extremely volatile.
Consequently, all of us suffered, as exemplified in the time
Dad beat me with a cue stick until it broke. Margaret,
however, was the special target of his venomous cruelty. His
special nickname for her was "Hitler," because of his belief
that she was domineering toward the rest of us. Once when

she was thirteen years old he angrily pummeled her with his
fists, screaming that she was old enough to be beaten like a
man. Most of the time my mother watched such proceedings
without interfering, but at times she openly abetted Dad in
the abuse.

My parents' fights had become so frequent and so violent
that my mother slept with a loaded pistol under her pillow.
On one particular occasion Dad arrived home in the wee
hours of the morning after another night of philandering.
As usual, his homecoming signaled another outbreak of
hostilities. This skirmish was just heating up when I heard
Mom tauntingly dare, "Go ahead and shoot, John!" The
challenge was evidently accepted because a shot echoed
throughout the house.

Cynthia and Michael lay whimpering in their beds, too
frightened to do otherwise, but Margaret raised the window
in her room, climbed out, and ran down the street, certain
that we would be the next victims. As for me, I simply lay in
bed wondering which parent had been shot. I really didn't
care. I thought that if either parent was dead conditions were
bound to improve. I didn't bother to investigate; it made no
difference to me.

It happened that nobody got shot and no explanation was
ever offered. Whether the gun was fired accidentally or Dad
was trying to scare Mom into cowering docility, I never
learned. Years were to pass before I found out how much
danger all of us were subjected to by the presence of that
weapon.

My parents' warfare did not hinder in the least their social
entertaining. Our house was often the scene of decadent
parties, always planned around some vulgar theme. Liquor
and drugs were as plentiful as water, and those were some of
the less suggestive items available. The house would be in
shambles following one of those group gropes, and we
children were expected to tidy up things.

Today, with accounts of child abuse in every newspaper,
it seems less bizarre that an eleven year old could be so

indifferent to the possibility of a parent's death or could even desire that death. At that time I knew nothing of such things. I only knew that we were trapped in a hellish vortex that confined us to a wretched existence and would ultimately result in even greater tragedy. Then and there I determined that I would not wait around for the catastrophic ending. I would pull myself out by the age of eighteen, and if I could find a way to escape before then, that would be all the better.

My parents were engrossed in their own selfish lives, so bare attention was given to the wants of their children, particularly their emotional needs. We received no individual quality time from either one, no interest was shown in our progress in school, and little supervision was given to our activities. As a result, I became incorrigible in my own behavior. I smoked my first cigarette at the age of eleven, and before I turned thirteen I had become a nicotine addict. I couldn't quit smoking if I wanted to, and I certainly didn't want to. I became more daring at shoplifting and even filled orders for others. My vocabulary was filthy, but I never uttered a foul word that I did not first hear my parents speak.

Paradoxically, I was not a rude, disrespectful child. I gave no problems at school and maintained a courteous attitude toward others. Yet even though I made friends easily, I preferred to be alone most of the time. A mold of fierce independence was being formed for me, and I easily slipped into it. It fit perfectly but was not at all comfortable. The depression upon me was so heavy that sometimes when I was alone I would suddenly burst into tears. There was no one to encourage me.

The only radiance breaking through my enshrouding darkness was music. I loved to sing and seized every opportunity to participate in singing groups at school. Even that window was closed, however, when my parents failed to provide the assistance necessary to develop whatever ability I had.

My feeling of inadequacy was reinforced by Mom's obvious favoritism of Margaret. She justified her position by the claim that she was just trying to counterbalance the hatred and abuse that Dad heaped upon Margaret. Conversely, he claimed to treat Margaret in such a desultory fashion because of Mom's partiality to her. Explanations were of little concern to me when what I craved was affection for its own sake.

The most poignant memory I have from this period is of a rare quiet evening when my father was watching a newscast. I sat beside him and playfully began to tease his beard. "Dad, I love you," I spoke softly with genuine emotion. The only acknowledgment on his part was to push me aside without even a break in his staring at the television.

A devastating sickness churned in my stomach and was replaced by a cold hardness that gripped me completely, promising to shield me from further injury as a result of rejection. I quietly left my father's side and slipped away. He wasn't any more aware of my absence than he was of my presence. It was the last time I ever told him that I loved him.

All of these memories rushed into my mind as I reflected upon my father's rekindled interest in me. Miracles might still happen, but somehow I could not accept my father's transformation from the man who ignored his eleven-year-old daughter's whisper of love into the man who was suddenly attentive and had taken me dancing. I was soon to learn that my skepticism was well founded.

# 4

November 1978
Fort Polk, Louisiana

I want to forget Fort Polk for many reasons, at the same time I can never forget it for the same reasons. Basic training was behind me, and I hoped that I was leaving some other things as well back at Fort Gordon. I never expected Army life to be a breeze, but the difficulties I encountered were vastly different from what I had anticipated.

Adjustment to the discomfort of a disciplined lifestyle had presented few problems to me, and I could contend with the physical and mental challenges offered by boot camp. I was totally unprepared, however, to deal with the exasperating harassment to which I was incessantly subjected. The sarcastic references to a woman's place in a man's Army, the stock jokes denigrating womanhood, and other forms of verbal barrage, while tediously irksome, could be stoically endured by the female recruits. There was, however, a far nastier victimization in the form of sexual bullying.

There seemed to be two stereotyped images of a woman soldier: she was either a butch displaying her manliness or a loose lassie hot to trot. While both are found in the military, it would be a gross generalization to fit the majority of women into these categories. Nevertheless we were constantly exposed to sexual harassment that ranged from filthy remarks to gang rapes.

I had enough street savvy to handle the junior league sexual innuendoes, but the cruder forms of vexation were more formidable. I regularly had to fight off impassioned males, mostly by caustic insults or artful cunning. One night I was the victim of an attempted rape, but escaped by telling the attacker that I was aroused but could respond with more enthusiasm the next night when I wasn't so tired. I actually convinced him of my sincerity.

The noncoms were often more difficult. There was a

certain lecherous drill instructor at Fort Gordon whom we
referred to as the Goat, indicative of his bestial nature. He
was always arranging duty assignments so that at least one of
the female recruits would have to spend some time with him
privately. It finally came to be my turn. I pulled an all-night
shift with this man as assistant Charge of Quarters. It proved
to be the toughest guard duty I ever experienced. I spent the
whole night defending myself against the rather forceful and
lewd proposals of the ruttish Sgt. Goat.

Filled with livid rage, I determined to do something about
it. Every other woman in the company had the same
repelling experience as I, so together we complained
through channels all the way to the battalion commander. As
a result, Sgt. Goat was reprimanded and reduced in rank.
Additionally, I earned a reputation for being uncooperative,
but I had no regrets.

Like so many other men who came on to me, the Goat was
married. Because of my earlier experiences in Maine, I vowed
never again to get involved with a married man. I wanted a
man who would be committed to me, and a married man on
the make is incapable of being committed, otherwise he
would honor the commitment made to his wife.

I arrived at Fort Polk late one night tired after the jolting
trip from Georgia. Wearily I trudged into the supply depot
expecting to receive from the clerk there the same gutter gab
with which everyone else addressed women recruits. Instead
I was treated with a courtesy that bordered on gallantry, and,
momentarily checking my resolve concerning married men,
determined to remember the name of Mark Snyder.

My two roommates and I had a relationship that was
considerably less than compatible. My private names for them
were "Smut" and "Snot"; one was a smutty lesbian and the
other was a snotty narcissist with the frosty sociability of a
codfish. What their appellation was for me I never learned,
but I'm sure it was equally complimentary.

The situation became intolerable in a matter of days, and
I had to escape. An opportunity came when Tony, another

soldier in our company, invited me to share a room with him in an oversized mobile home inhabited by three other men. I figured that living with four men, even if I did have to share a room with one of them, was far better than losing my sanity or being charged with murder. So I agreed, with the clear understanding that no payment would be given other than my part of the rent and utilities.

I had dated Tony a few times and had resisted his aggressive advances simply because I had no interest in him. Out of boredom I had even spent a weekend with him off base and had successfully fended off his desperate overtures. Tony must have truly loved me because every night for two months I slept in the same bed with the man and not once did he touch me. I noticed, however, that he was showing more signs of frustration and was beginning to close the distance between us in bed. My unconventional living arrangements came to an abrupt conclusion when Tony, enraged at the growing relationship that I had developed with Mark Snyder, kicked me out.

When I moved into Tony's trailer, I was delighted to discover that Mark lived directly across from us. We had frequent encounters over the previous weeks, and I knew that he and his wife were separated. He never failed to treat me with respect, and I was comfortable in his presence.

He soon became a frequent visitor to our place, and we would all get high together. Sometimes he would spend the night when the utilities at his trailer were cut off for lack of payment. Instead of recognizing an obvious lack of responsibility, I began to return Mark's visits, staying longer each time.

Tony's eruption came after I had spent two consecutive nights at Mark's, sleeping on the couch. Moving was no problem. I simply transferred my belongings to the mobile home across the lane where Mark gladly received me. Our relationship remained platonic for a week. One night Mark was in the bedroom gathering his things in preparation for sleeping on the couch. "Mark," I called after him, "you don't have to sleep on the couch." He turned and came back into the room, closing the door.

My live-in association with Mark began in January 1979, and we planned to be married when his divorce was finalized. Meanwhile, by the time summer arrived, Army life, particularly the harassment, had become almost unbearable. Perhaps it was the preview of being a housewife that I was receiving that changed my attitude toward the Army; whatever the reason, I wanted out.

When I voiced my discontent to the commander, however, he persuaded me to exercise a little more patience. To ease the situation he offered me an opportunity to go on a TDY (temporary duty) mission in Mississippi to support a National Guard training exercise. "It will be like a paid vacation," was his promise.

Some vacation! For the trip to Mississippi I was paired with a libidinous Casanova who had a raunchy reputation to maintain. For four solid hours I was bombarded with kinky suggestions and actual physical demonstrations by this epicurean playboy. My failure to respond positively to his crude performance set the tone for the rest of the mission.

I was the only woman on the team, already labeled "uncooperative," and for the full ten days of the maneuvers I was given the most undesirable tasks and was left in the field without relief while the men relaxed. In spite of my cruel treatment, I somehow sensed that the excessive fatigue which I felt, compounded by my sullen anger, had a contributing factor other than laborious toil. At the time I had no way of knowing that I was pregnant, especially since I had my regular period during the week.

To my surprise, word of the maltreatment against me reached the officials at Fort Polk. Typical of the Army, however, no action was taken against the offenders, neither the free-loving lady killer nor the lazy-legged do-nothings in the field. The report served only to add to my misery, resulting in even heavier duty assignments.

After several weeks I knew for certain that I was pregnant but couldn't convince anyone else. For some reason, I tested negative going into my fourth month of pregnancy; thus, goldbricking was added to my reputation. My duty assignments became even more burdensome, and I knew that I had to leave the Army before I broke.

In September 1979, before I could apply for a discharge, Mark's divorce became final. We were married the next day. My wedding was somewhat different from that of Charles and Di. Instead of a gleaming cathedral and a storied castle, there was a decrepit general store on the edge of a Louisiana swamp. In place of a priest, resplendent in multicolored vestments, standing before an ornate altar, there was the store proprietor who doubled as a justice of the peace, garbed in faded overalls, and standing on the other side of the rough-plank counter.

Rather than a retinue of beautiful and rich young attendants, our witness was a grizzled elderly backwoods customer whose entrance happened to coincide with our own. The dried snuff juice on his chin added character to his smile. I had no wedding gown of smooth satin and delicate lace but wore the best camouflage fatigues the Army could offer, even if they were tight because of a slight protrusion at my waist.

Substituting for the lofty swell of notes ascending from an organ was the harmony of a droning mosquito and a buzzing fly. The intoxicating fragrance of a sea of brightly hued flowers was replaced by the mingled scents of molasses, chicory, pickles, tobacco, and similar items. We didn't hear the ringing of thousands of bells heralding a celebration, but we were treated to the solitary chime of the cash register as our officiating justice rang up the $5 fee. No champagne was available for a toast, but our rustic witness popped a couple of bottles of Dr Pepper and insisted on paying. He didn't ask to kiss the bride, an oversight for which the bride was grateful.

No carriage awaited us to be drawn by magnificent
prancing horses, but we did step over two dozing hounds to
get to our car. We weren't whisked away to a secluded love
nest; we simply returned to the trailer park. All in all, it was
a memorable wedding, slapstick in every detail.

It didn't take me long to discover that I had married an
immature and selfish man who was totally irresponsible.
There had been plenty of warning signs all during our
premarital relationship, but love in my case was not only
blind but also devoid of all senses.

At first I was enthralled by Mark's lackadaisical,
devil-may-care attitude, but his character flaws soon drove
an immovable wedge between us. It wasn't just his drinking
and use of hard drugs that bothered me. They were only
symptoms of an irresponsible and inconsiderate temperament
that allowed no impelling motivation or industrious drive.

I had sung the old familiar tune "He'll Change after We're
Married" until I was convinced it was an irrefutable truth.
Like myriads of others, however, I soon discovered that an
unspoken addendum to the "I do" of the wedding vow was
"when it pleases me." Faults so easily overlooked before
marriage become monstrous millstones afterwards. When the
veil of gossamery stardust is snatched from the bride's eyes,
she can see clearly that the shining armor was tarnished all
along, and that Prince Charming never really was anything
but a toad.

It's a humbling discovery to find that you really don't have
the power to change another person's nature. Even the magic
of marriage is impotent in conjuring spells that transform
darkness into light. Unfortunately, wedlock is no lock at all
against certain forces and provides no security against the
pain of disappointment and disillusionment.

Too soon I was jolted with the stark realization that Mark
cared little for me or the baby that I was carrying. As soon
as my pregnancy was confirmed, I stopped smoking both
marijuana and cigarettes, a decision that soured me to Mark.
According to him, I was no longer any fun, and both he and

his drug-hooked friends charged me with a holier-than-thou attitude. As a consequence, Mark preferred the company of his friends and became more deeply involved in heavy drugs. I spent many lonely nights while he partied, and the rare occasions when I accompanied him usually resulted in humiliating scenes in which he belittled me mercilessly.

Two homespun philosophers from the county seat Spit 'n Whittle Club were once discussing the soaring divorce rate. "Looks to me like a little common sense would prevent a lot of divorces," opined one. To which the other rejoined, "Looks to me like a little common sense would prevent a lot of marriages."

Why did I marry the type of man that I did? Simply stated, heart overruled head. I was eighteen years old when I met and later moved in with Mark Snyder, and I merely superimposed my own idealistic impression of what I wanted him to be upon the reality of what he was. Every girl, no matter who or what she is, draws her own image of ideal manhood. When a likely candidate approaches, it's ridiculously easy to see only what you want to see and to deny the obvious. To me, Mark, of all the men I had ever known, was the most chivalrous.

When I became involved with Mark, I knew little of the biblical teachings concerning morality and still less of scriptural principles concerning marriage. In all likelihood it would have made no difference in my actions anyway. Certainly I had no parental guidance in such matters, either by oral teaching or personal example. I honestly think that if my father, whose dislike of Mark was immediate and apparent, had intervened with sincere paternal concern and solid counsel, I may have heard warning signals. Where Mark was concerned, however, there were only murmurings, never sagacious advice.

Dad met Mark early in August 1979, during a brief leave we took first in Maryland, visiting Mark's family, and then in Norfolk. Although he was formally civil, Dad made no special effort to conceal his hostility. I foolishly attributed his attitude to the reluctance a father naturally feels when he is about to lose his daughter to marriage.

For two days I delayed informing my father that I would have to leave the Army because I was pregnant. As it turned out, I didn't have to; he had already guessed the situation. He told me that it really wasn't difficult to surmise the truth. Every time he attempted to discuss my Army career, my bottom lip began to quiver and I quickly changed the subject. Dad was right. I was terribly fearful of disappointing him after his high hopes for me.

Despite what he had just learned, however, my father in no way accepted my decision to seek a discharge from the Army. The very next day he took Mark and me to Fort Story, a small Army base located at Cape Henry in Virginia Beach, where he had arranged for us to meet with a certain officer.

Supposedly this officer had something to do with determining the duty stations to which recruits were assigned. The express intimation was that I could be stationed anywhere I chose, a privilege calculated to keep me in the Army. Dad also openly assured me that the officer could take care of the problem concerning sexual harassment. How the man could do all that, I never knew. Nor did I know how my father's influence extended to him, but based on Dad's past performance I believed that it could happen. Anyway, nothing was said or done in the meeting to change my mind.

Dad still had one more pitch to make in his attempt to persuade me to pursue a career in the Army. The day after our visit to Fort Story, he asked me to accompany him alone to Knickerbocker's, a restaurant/bar located on Little Creek Road in Norfolk.

After we had settled into an isolated booth and ordered a gin and tonic for him and red wine for me, he bluntly opened the conversation with a straightforward and intriguing statement: "I want to talk to you about something so illegal that even discussing it with me could make you an accessory. If you don't want to hear it, say so and the conversation will go no further. On the other hand, your consent to listen

will obligate you to maintain the strictest confidence,
regardless of what you decide to do after you hear me.
With that understanding, which will it be?"

I had a feeling it didn't matter much what I wanted to do.
I was well acquainted with my father's glib and cajoling
manner and knew that I was no match for him, especially
when he was bent on turning things to his own advantage. At
any rate, the fascination of being privy to something so
mysterious was too alluring to resist.

To be honest, ever since I had been old enough to
understand anything at all about the Navy's pay scale, I had
wondered where my father got the money that allowed the
extravagance that he so obviously enjoyed. Once I even
remarked to him that anybody who could afford to live like
he did must be involved in something illegal. At that time he
merely laughed and dismissed it as a joke.

At times I would engage in half-serious speculations about
the source of Dad's income, but not having been around him
much since the divorce, I had not dwelt on it. Now the most
convincing conclusion came rushing back to me as I fleetingly
recalled the frequent sudden trips that Dad would take
without any explanation. I was positive that he was a drug
dealer, and that is what I expected to hear as I nodded my
consent for him to proceed.

He began by describing his early years of struggle in the
Navy and how the burden of providing for his family caused
him to consider leaving the service. His brother, my Uncle
Art, convinced him of the foolishness involved in giving up
what he had attained. A vague reference to the time frame
led me to place it to the time that we were living in Ladson.

Then without warning, he asked me if I would risk a
two-year prison sentence for $10,000. Before I could
respond, he began a harangue about how I was already in
prison, since the Army was one huge prison camp. Much
of what he said made sense to me, especially when he
portrayed the Army as a system meant to exploit its weak
members, which could be turned to the advantage of those

strong enough to beat the system. I had both observed and
experienced enough in my brief military career to understand
his point.

"Look at the service as a great opportunity to make
money," he told me. "I've made plenty of money out of my
Navy career." Without preamble, he proceeded to tell me
that if I could procure classified information, he had a buyer
for it. The vague implication was that he had been involved in
such dealings for years. There was no explanation, defense,
hint of remorse, or suggestion of apology. It was just a cold,
matter-of-fact announcement of a routine business deal;
however, he did not identify the recipients of the material he
was selling. Nor did it occur to me at the time to ask how
he was now obtaining secret documents; he had retired from
the Navy a couple of years before. He never hinted that
others were involved with him.

The pedestrian manner in which my father fed me
this information made his illegal activities sound more like
an innocent prank than an unpardonable treachery that
threatened the national security. He confirmed this
impression by assuring me that a lot of people were doing the
same thing, so I might as well get some of the same benefits.

I was beginning to see the logic of what he was saying.
Basically it was this: every business or organization, and even
society itself, is a system designed to screw you, so it's up to
you to turn the screw the other way. How does an office
worker justify the fact that he uses company stationery and
postage for personal correspondence or appropriates pens and
staplers for his or his family's use? That's just the way the
system works. You aren't paid or appreciated enough, so
you'll make it up whatever way you can, and that usually
involves screwing the company.

The same principle causes a policeman to go on the take
or to look the other way; a politician to legislate profligate
bills so full of pork that they squeal when handled; an
industrialist to pilfer his competitor's secrets; an honest
citizen to color his income-tax return; and writers of books to

capitalize on the theme of looking out for oneself and shafting the other guy before he stabs you. Essentially it's a basic and accepted formula that is practiced every day. With that reasoning, my father's crime was such that words like "spy" and "traitor" were out of place.

When it was my turn to talk, I was full of objections. "I'm in no position to obtain information that would be of value to anyone." No problem. Strings could be pulled to assure me of a choice assignment. My part would be to continue to maintain an outstanding record and receive promotions. I would soon be entrusted with a position in a major military communications center where I would have access to top-secret material.

"But I'm pregnant." Have an abortion. That suggestion I adamantly refused, so my father assured me that I could take medical leave.

"How can I keep Mark from knowing?" It's a simple matter to keep secrets from your mate, and Dad considered himself an expert in that area. He would teach me how to hide my money in such a way that I could enjoy its benefits without Mark's knowledge.

I have to admit that it was exciting to have been entrusted with my father's secret. My immediate desire was to agree to do what he wanted because I knew it would win his approval. He realized how much I wanted him to be a part of my life, so he carefully stressed the fact that we would be partners, sharing an adventure together.

Dad didn't press me for an immediate answer. Had he insisted that I make a decision then and there, the results could have been frightful. As it was, I left the restaurant confused, with my emotions fiercely churning in conflict. By the end of the day my deadly internal struggle intensified to the point that I could no longer contain it. I felt that I had to share the turmoil with Mark and solicit his counsel. That decision was one of many mistakes I would make, and later it proved to be disastrous.

# 5

## August 1979
## Interstate 95 between
## Virginia and Louisiana

I leaned wearily against the door of the car as Mark and I rocketed toward Louisiana from Virginia. With him behind the wheel, a faster word than "speed" is needed. Right then I didn't care; I wanted to distance myself as far and as fast as I could from my father. I was still shaken by his revelation to me, and confiding in Mark had only served to intensify the disquietude that was steadily tightening its hold on me.

Telling Mark about Dad's proposal had been a dreadful error in judgment on my part. He had exploded in a patriotic tirade against traitors in general and my blankety-blank father in particular, screaming murderous threats against him. I was petrified, not only at the thought of what Mark might attempt against Dad, but at the vision of what my father might do to me if he learned that I had violated his confidence.

I was gripped in the clutches of an inescapable dilemma, afraid that whatever decision I made would be displeasing to myself or to Mark or to my father. At the moment I hated the man who had put me in such an intolerable position, yet I was strangely tantalized by the mystery surrounding him.

Blocking out the deafening yowl of heathenish rock music blaring from the radio, I reflected on the shocking conversation that had caused my plight. The chief point in my father's sales pitch to me was the expression of his desire to help me get into the "mainstream of America." I thought it ironic that he was poisoning the stream he wanted me to get into. It didn't make sense to me that he could enjoy the so-called good life while at the same time he was engaging in activities calculated to destroy the structure that fostered that kind of prosperity.

As I pondered this riddle, I was hit by the abrupt realization that my father had been setting me up from the moment he offered to pay for the courses that were necessary for my completing high school. I reviewed with disgust his pretended concern for me since the time he learned of my intention to enter the Army—and communications at that. The purpose of the inquisition at Fort Gordon concerning the equipment I used became clear.

I envisioned my father compiling notes, summarizing what he had learned from me, and passing them on to his contact, along with information about his newest recruit possibility—his own daughter. He had a golden pipeline in the making and was certain that he could manipulate me into doing his bidding. All he had to do was to dangle his love before me like candy just out of reach. What I wanted most was to win both his love and his approval, but he had put an exorbitant price on both.

"America's mainstream," as my father described it, was a placid easy-flowing watercourse without any waves of financial distress rocking the boat or any indigent rapids in narrow straits swamping the vessel. I suppose he never considered the fact that he was on an aimless pleasure cruise. If he really wanted to help me, where had he been all the years before? Why was there no offer to put me though college or a vo-tech school?

The answer was patently clear. John Walker was much too self-seeking to allow himself to extend charity to anyone else unless it served his own avarice. His benevolence to me flowed not from a noble heart of genuine magnanimity, but rather from a strong heart of self-aggrandizement. I shuddered at the realization that my father was a traitor two times over, to his country and to me, and I felt his treason far more keenly as a daughter than as a citizen. Could he really be so unsparingly callous?

Indeed he could. If there was any doubt, a brief consideration of our family history since the late sixties would bring confirmation. The understanding that I received based on the unveiling of my father's secret was like the proverbial missing piece of the puzzle. The baffling complications in

our household suddenly found explanation with the use of
the interpretative key now in my possession.

Now I knew how we could afford to discard a small trailer
behind the Bamboo Snack Bar in favor of a high-rise luxury
apartment. Not only did the reason for the sudden and
striking reversal of our financial situation become clear, but
the cause of the fighting and constant tension that had totally
disrupted our family life was clarified.

I had no way of knowing the extent of my mother's
awareness of Dad's activities, but the beginning of her
personal disintegration coincided with that of the entire
family. In addition, I recalled derogatory comments about
my father that she had made through the years but which
didn't make sense to me at the time they were spoken. Now
stripped of their shroud of mystery, they were unmistakably
clear.

A consuming anger suffused me at the realization that it
was my father's greedy selfishness that had caused us to
endure such a nightmarish hell over the past few years.
While he denied himself nothing in pursuing a profligate
lifestyle, he watched his family die an agonizing death.
Refusing to yield to the gentle persuasion of the motion of
the car to drift into sleep, I focused on some of the more
distasteful incidents in the family circle.

The family moved from San Diego in 1971 to Union City,
California, a suburb of San Francisco. As had been the
pattern of our last two moves, we acquired a larger, more
expensive house. As it was, housing turned out to be the only
extra benefit the family gained from the payments my father
received from his illegal activities. Everything else he
lavished upon himself. In fact, my mother went to work at a
nearby fast-food restaurant to provide the basic necessities for
the rest of the family.

Dad was at sea for long periods of time, and when he was
home he kept himself apart from the family, constantly
carousing with his friends and other women. It was scarcely

better with my mother. Her alcoholism had advanced to the
stage that she was most always drunk when she was home.

   We children were totally without parental guidance
concerning value systems. Things might have been different
had we been steered toward wholesome activities and friends.
At least we could have tasted a normal childhood; however,
we had no one except each other and a few friends (who were
on the same wavelength). Dad simply didn't want to be
bothered with the process of overseeing the development of
his children, and Mom simply couldn't do it alone.

   The time that we lived in Union City was the most difficult
time that I had endured. I was at the age when a blooming
girl most needs a strong relationship with a caring and
understanding mother, and my own mother was incapable of
fulfilling the role. She was out drinking almost every evening
with one of her girlfriends, often not even bothering to come
home. When she was home she spent her time drinking and
berating us. Whatever guilt she felt was transferred to us.
She blamed us for her alcoholism, and she was very
successful in placing blame on us. Watching her degenerate
month after month, I began to feel increasingly guilty for
her deterioration. Somehow I believed that I was responsible
for her condition.

   My mother's violent outbursts became more frequent and
more physical. Daily screaming matches were quite normal,
but her hysteria was often displayed in unrestrained savagery,
and it made no difference where we were at the time. On
one occasion I displeased her by being outside talking with
friends when she got home. Without warning she grabbed me
by the hair and yanked me to the ground. She began to kick
me, cursing and screaming. The scene was repeated when I
escaped to the inside of the house, except this time she
pounded my head with her shoe. I was beginning to fade into
unconsciousness when, out of breath, she stopped the
beating. I'm convinced that only her weariness saved my life.
When I managed to rouse myself from the floor, all she said
was, "Fix me a drink." Not then or later has there been an

acknowledgment in any way of what happened—no inquiry concerning my well-being and no apology either for nearly beating me to death or for humiliating me before the neighborhood.

Mom's alcoholic rage found expression in other ways as well. Once she forced Michael to bend over a garbage can and shoved his head down into the stinking, rotting filth, holding him there as his gagging mouth filled with the putrid mess. On another occasion she stripped Cynthia naked and whipped her with a belt while Margaret and I were made to watch. Knowing Cynthia's extreme modesty, she then ordered her to go outside for the whole neighborhood to gawk at. Only our intervention spared our sister further shame.

The character that my sisters and I were developing was already bent out of shape. Now Michael was following the pattern. We could not expect otherwise, given the total absence of moral values in the home. He was in constant trouble at school, and his only interest was rock music. To pacify him, our parents gave him a drum set. He would sit in his room for hours at a time, beating his drums in accompaniment to taped music. His particular hero was the bizarre Alice Cooper, and by patterning himself after such an occultic figure, Michael was definitely heading in the wrong direction. He had plenty of company though.

Unbelievable as it may sound, even my dad's pet German shepherd, Sailor, was turned into a neurotic bundle of fur by the maddening environment in which he lived. His case of jitters soon turned into violent aggression, and he attacked both members of the family and others in the neighborhood. Mom refused to get rid of the dog because she was fearful of my father's reaction. Someone finally called the police, and they took him away. I still bear a few scars to remind me of Sailor.

With a home situation like this, I stayed away from it as much as possible. As an eleven year old I had already begun a pattern of running away a few months before we moved to Union City. Now that I was twelve I became both bolder and

wiser in my absences. Sometimes I would stay at a friend's
house, but most often I would hide in the woods for days at a
time, with food provided by confidantes. Even when I wasn't
on the run, I was on the streets day and night, usually in the
company of my closest friend, Dori. It was with her that I
began smoking marijuana and became streetwise.

My recalcitrant attitude widened the breach between me
and my parents. For my part, I was bedeviled by their failure
to show any concern about my needs and feelings. Not once
during this difficult period did either of my parents make an
attempt to communicate with me in an effort to uncork the
pent-up emotions fermenting inside me. As far as they were
concerned, I was an ungrateful brat incapable of showing
them respect. My father churlishly described me as "a
smart-assed bitch biting the hand that feeds her."

I contemplated suicide. It's difficult to unravel the tangled
thoughts that trouble the mind of a potential suicide victim of
any age, but the misery of a twelve-year-old reject such as I
was is so uncomplicated that it needs no analysis. To me the
picture was clear. Life was a drag that didn't promise to
get any better, and existence in such lousy circumstances
wasn't even worth the effort of getting up in the morning
and getting dressed. For me every day ended as it
began—hopeless. Anything beyond that is for psychologists to
expound on.

There was no lengthy premeditation in what I did, nor was
it a spur-of-the-moment act precipitated by a family quarrel,
boyfriend problems, or any such thing. It was merely a sober
and calculated decision to give up.

One evening when my father was away at sea, my mother
was out drinking, and my brother and sisters were watching
television, I went into my parents' room. There were five
guns in a bedside table drawer, all loaded. Selecting a silver
revolver with pearl handles, I sat on the floor with my back
against the bed.

I had no thoughts of gate crashing heaven, of inflicting
punishment either upon myself or others, or of subjecting

myself to martyrdom for some cause. Although I feared
no pain, I was saddened by the finality of it all and was
distressed at the thought that no one would care.

I was crying as I held the gun to my head and began to
squeeze the trigger. I could feel the movement of the trigger
as the pressure increased and knew the hammer was being
cocked. All of a sudden, my finger was paralyzed and
absolutely refused to respond to its nerve signal to move. A
spasm of terror shuddered through my body. I fled to my
room in an uncontrollable panic, feeling as though I had just
locked myself in with a company of unseen demons sent to
destroy me.

For weeks following this abortive attempt at self-
destruction, I was plagued with diabolic urgings to try
it again, but the memory of the terror that had possessed
me precluded any further effort. Nor did I share with anyone
what had happened.

Years later I read that more than two million teenagers in
this country attempt suicide each year, and that more than six
thousand of them succeed. I came very near to being a part
of the 1973 statistics and can only believe that the hand of
God was clasped over mine, preventing me from blowing
myself into eternity.

My father no longer made an effort to conceal his
dissipated lifestyle from his children. One evening in 1973
after he returned from Hong Kong, he announced that he
was going to treat us to a scenic slide show of his trip. The
pictures consisted of a few panoramic views of Hong Kong,
but most of them featured prostitutes, some not much older
than I, in various poses. Some of them were standing
enticingly in front of their establishments, with prices for
various services plainly visible.

Later my mother found some lewd pictures that Dad had
not shared with us. She showed them to me so that I would
"know just what a scum he really is." The pictures were
sexual scenes involving my father and young Oriental girls.

Not long after this episode, Dad called while he was away

on duty and told us to prepare for a move back to Norfolk
because he was being transferred there. It was then that
Mom confided that she was going to divorce him and that we
would remain in California. I was elated. I had no desire to
return to Virginia, but mostly I felt that we might at least
salvage something of our lives. Perhaps Mom would overcome
her alcoholism. She had only an eighth-grade education but
was blessed with keen intelligence. Despite her alcoholic
condition, her abilities were such that she had been named
manager at the hamburger place where she worked. I was
convinced we could survive on our own.

My optimism was short-lived. Immediately upon my
father's return, he and Mom went into the den to talk.
When they came out after only a few minutes, the look of
resignation on Mom's face told me that nothing had changed.
I was furious at my mother for her weakness in flinging away
our opportunity to escape this bondage that had enslaved us,
and I was angry at my father for whatever hold he had over
Mom. "He promised to change," was her bland explanation.
I didn't believe it, and I knew that she didn't. Since my father
preferred a lifestyle more suitable to a bachelor
unencumbered by family entanglements, why would he not
readily agree to a divorce?

Several years were to pass before Mom enlightened me
concerning a portion of the discussion in the den. Dad said
that because of her alcoholism he was certain to gain custody
of the children if a divorce was executed. He would
immediately place us in foster homes. That in itself would
not have deterred her.

Now, several years later, I understood the situation better,
having learned of my father's clandestine activities. It also
explained why he didn't seize the opportunity to be free of
us. In spite of his hatred for his wife and the restrictions that
his family placed upon him, his fear of discovery forced him
to maintain control over the family. His alcoholic wife shared
the secret of his double life and could expose him at any time.
It was better to keep her around so he could control her.

I knew nothing of these matters at the time. So I expressed my anger in the same way I had shown dissatisfaction for the past two years—I ran away. As usual it wasn't long before I was back, but this time my return was different. My father exploded and announced his intention to discipline me. In a way, I was inwardly glad for the punishment, because it indicated that in some measure he still cared for me.

Yet even that hope was momentary; Dad hastened to assure me that he could not care less if I stayed or left and that I was free to leave at anytime, on the condition that I not come back. The beating was to be administered to me because I was disgracing the family in acting as I did. It was ironic that he was true to his selfish nature even in dishing out corporal punishment. His concern was not for my welfare, but for his own standing.

I was smarting with such inner fury that I was oblivious to the pain of the heavy belt stinging my body, even when blood spurted from places where my flesh had been broken. With hissing sarcasm I challenged him: "What right do you have to discipline me? You don't even know me, much less understand me." He accepted the expression of disdain with a plaintive admission: "You're right, I don't know you."

At that moment, I felt that our future as a family unit was hanging precariously on his next step. If there was any acceptance of guilt or the barest hint of remorse, perhaps we would have a chance to survive. When he turned and walked away after only a slight hesitation, I knew that love had lost the battle to win my father back to his family. So I cried. I cried as never before, with tears coming from my very soul. My grief didn't come from the physical pain that had just been inflicted upon me, but from the throb of memory as I realized for certain that there would be no more family laughter. There had indeed been joyous days long ago when Dad had given himself to us. Something had stolen him from us, and we would never have him again.

Any doubt that we were through as a family was dispelled as we drove cross-country to Virginia towing a sleek sailboat behind our equally attractive van. My father was a stranger performing an unpleasant task and made no attempt to conceal his contempt. Mom was not well and had been hemorrhaging repeatedly for several months. During the trip she again began to hemorrhage. Dad pulled into the nearest rest area, turned to her with a look of revulsion, and made the sardonic comment, "Clean it up, Barbara!" There was no demonstration of concern or patient sympathy. Later, when the van began swaying across all lanes because of a blown tire on the boat trailer, I entertained the desire that we would all be killed in a fiery crash, as long as no other car would be involved. I just wanted the charade to be over.

No housing arrangements had been made prior to our arrival in Norfolk in August 1973, so the six of us spent thirty days in a cheap room in a Navy hostel which contained only two double beds, a couch, a bathroom, and a tiny kitchen area. My father, too selfish to spend more money on his family than necessity dictated, refused to secure more adequate accommodations. It still could have worked if he and Mom had shared a bed. Then the three girls could have slept in the other bed while Michael took the couch. Instead, Dad insisted on sleeping with Michael. That left Mom and one girl on the other bed, another girl on the couch, and the third girl on the floor.

The tension in the overcrowded room was like a rubber band stretched to its limit, and more than once it broke in an outburst of violence. One particular eruption happened at dinner one night when Dad, displeased with Cynthia, purposefully arose from the table, walked over to her, and without warning punched her in the mouth with his fist, sending her crashing into the corner. The blow itself was bad enough, but its effect was worsened by the fact that Cynthia was wearing braces. No one dared to speak as she lay whimpering on the floor, with blood pouring from inside her lacerated mouth.

During most of that hellish month my mother was in a state of nervous paroxysm. Sometimes she would sit for hours, oblivious to everything about her, staring vacantly at empty

## ERRATA

On page 85, the last line on the page was inadvertantly left off. The paragraph should read:


I was at a high pitch of excitement all the way across the country, an euphoria doubly blissful because of my declaration of independence. I was finally free and was enjoying every delicious moment of my liberty—that is, until I neared the end of my journey in Oakland, California.

space. She definitely needed professional attention, but all my father did was sneer at her in disgust. He was totally unfeeling.

The ordeal wasn't as dreadful to Margaret and me. We simply vanished every day and smoked ourselves into such a silly stupor on pot that we felt ourselves largely unaffected by the bummed-out situation in the hostel.

Soon after we moved into the house on Old Ocean View Road in Norfolk, all pretense was dropped. Communication between my parents was practically nonexistent, and it was essentially the same between parents and children. Margaret refused to accept Dad's brutality any more and ran away to California, where, at the age of seventeen and still in high school, she moved in with the older boyfriend she had left behind.

Margaret's example gave me the courage to leave, although it was not quite so simple as walking away. I had to get enough money for a bus ticket to California, where I hoped I could live with my friend, Dori. The fastest and most convenient way to get the money was to steal it, specifically from my father. His unvarying routine made it easy to systematically steal from his bedroom. On the evenings when he came home, he changed clothes, placing on the dresser the contents of his pockets, including his weighty money clip. Then he would withdraw to the seclusion of his den until he retired for the night. Almost every day I managed to take some money, sometimes as much as $50 at a time.

Finally the day came when I was ready to go. I walked out on the pretense of going to the store. In addition to the money I had accumulated, all I took with me was my purse and a few articles of clothing stuffed in a small bag. I was wearing shorts and sandals. At the age of fifteen I set out on my bold adventure.

I was at a high pitch of excitement all the way across the country, an euphoria doubly blissful because of my declaration of independence. I was finally free and was enjoying every delicious moment of my liberty—that is, until

I neared the end of my journey in OAKland, Calyornia

It was one o'clock in the morning and I would have to wait
in the practically deserted terminal for another five hours
before I could get a bus to Niles Canyon, where Dori lived.
The possibility that I would encounter danger in any form
had not even occurred to me, but now it presented itself in a
terribly frightening way.

Two men approached me, no doubt recognizing me for
the runaway that I was, and tried to persuade me to go with
them. When I was persistent in resisting their suggestions,
they resorted to coercion, and made ready to escort me out
of the building. A woman, seeing my plight, came to my
rescue. She said, "As soon as my son arrives, we'll take you
to your destination." She made the offer to me, but it was in
reality a statement of dismissal to the two baddies. Her tone
was gentle but authoritative, and the hooligans slithered
away.

Shortly thereafter her son arrived and they drove me all
the way to Dori's house. Not once did she refer to the fact
that I was a runaway. It was not to be the last time I saw her.

Dori's parents allowed me to stay only on the condition that
I call to inform Mom of my whereabouts. To this demand I
readily acceded, but when they also talked to my mother,
it was apparent that she did a snow job on them. They
completely swallowed my mother's story that everything was
roses at home, and that I was only an ungrateful rebellious
child. Anyway, Mom gave me consent to stay one month in
California.

Two weeks of that month I spent with Margaret and her
boyfriend in his tiny one-room apartment. I don't know why
girls often pick men just like their fathers, but Margaret
had a real loser, a selfish, abusive beach bum hooked on
pornography. One night they wanted to be alone, so they
took me to the home of an acquaintance of Margaret's
boyfriend. Why they left a fifteen-year-old girl in a house
alone with a horny twenty-eight-year-old man she had never
even met is beyond me.

I did absolutely nothing to stimulate him, but rather was
innocently watching inane game shows on television. All of a

sudden, he came on to me. Without speaking a single word, he pushed me to the floor and stripped me. At that time I was a virgin. I was so petrified with fear that I couldn't make a sound, and I certainly was no match for his strength. I could only close my eyes and steel myself with silent resistance as he forced himself on me. It was a brutal introduction to sexual experience. I was too scared to tell anyone what happened.

Shortly before my return to Norfolk, I received a surprise visit from the kind woman who had befriended me at the bus station. She told me that she knew I was a runaway and was concerned for my welfare. There was no mistaking the sincerity of her concern as she assured me that she would be praying for me. As far as I knew, not one person had ever prayed for me, and that woman, without hurling judgmental pronouncements against me or trying to cram anything down my throat, touched my life in a way completely unknown to her. She even wrote to me later and sent me an encouraging book on mother-daughter relationships. Perhaps it is to her prayers that I must attribute the fact that I was not discarded by God, but was selected for something more noble than I could envision.

If God had a plan for me, however, it must have been put on hold. The situation at Norfolk was the same in spite of my temporary attachment to a Baptist church. I continued to run away, once all the way to Wisconsin. On each occasion I expanded my education in the world's university, with classes offered on the streets.

Mom had enough; she had me arrested for being incorrigible. The time that I spent in the detention home was not entirely in vain. One day as I was sitting in my cell, I heard the strains of a popular song by Diana Ross. Its title was "Do You Know Where You're Going To?" As a matter of fact, I did know, and I didn't like it.

I opened my eyes when the car bounced over a rough spot on the pavement. I was surprised to find my face wet with tears.

# 6

## September 1980
## Leesville, Louisiana

I began building a castle in the air but wound up trying to pull myself out of the mud.

My pregnancy gave me a sense of warm satisfaction, especially since I experienced no discomfort. Life with Mark wasn't quite so easy, however. The problem wasn't so much that we fought, but we rarely took time to talk. Very early in our relationship he distanced himself from me, and I could never ascertain the cause. He showed little interest in the progress of my pregnancy and exhibited no anticipation whatever over the forthcoming birth of our baby. When I would suggest that he feel the baby kick, he would respond without enthusiasm. His laconic attitude of "That's nice, Honey," pierced me deeply. I earnestly wanted him to share my glowing excitement; instead, he was as apathetic as a total stranger.

Mark had begun to go out alone with his friends only a few weeks after our marriage, always coming home very late. I cried myself to sleep most nights, struggling to convince myself that our relationship would improve with the arrival of the baby. These evenings spent alone would have been unbearable had I foreseen how much wider the breach between us would become.

My father would have been delighted had he known my misery. Of all the people I knew, he took the greatest pleasure in being able to chortle, "I told you so!" Mostly for that reason I never gave him a hint about my troubled marriage.

Dad had come to Louisiana for a brief visit only two weeks after Mark and I returned from Norfolk. His main purpose was to press the matter of my staying in the Army and gaining access to classified material. He grasped at everything to curry my favor, and one offer drew an

immediate response from me. We desperately needed a car,
so I readily accepted Dad's suggestion that I come to Virginia
where he would be able to use his connections to get us a
fabulous deal. We agreed on a date early in September for
me to visit Norfolk.

A thousand-mile bus ride when you are three months
pregnant is not particularly enjoyable, but in my case it was
downright cushy in comparison to what lay ahead of me at
my destination. No one was at the bus terminal to meet
me. So I waited . . . and called . . . and waited some
more . . . and called again . . . and again. I waited for five
hours, making vain attempts to call both my father and my
sister, Margaret, who by this time was back in Norfolk living
with her boyfriend. I had spent the last of my money for food
during the night, sparing only one quarter. The fact that I
had not eaten anything all day made the bags of potato chips
in the beckoning vending machine even more tempting. My
quarter was caught in a powerful tug of war between the
telephone and the snack machine. The telephone, useless as it
had been, prevailed.

Taking a taxi to my father's house was out of the question;
I had no money. Finally, a man who had brought someone
to the station perceived my distress and offered to help. I
rejected the caution that automatically suggested itself to me
and gratefully allowed him to drive me to Dad's place. As I
expected, there was no one there. A cold rain was driving
across the bay by this time, and I was shivering. My shelter
for the next few hours was my father's pickup, which he had
left unlocked in the driveway. It was well after dark before I
finally reached Margaret's boyfriend from a neighbor's phone.

Dad returned late that night, having forgotten that I was
scheduled to arrive and having taken a joy trip out of town
with a lady friend. He never apologized nor even recognized
my inconvenience.

I spent a week with my father, during which time he
secured for me a beautiful foreign sports car for $150 a
month. Whatever gratification I felt from being the owner of

such an automobile was soured by Dad's unflagging efforts to recruit me as a supplier of secret documents. He was as zealous as a salesman, and my resistance almost crumbled before his constant pitches.

My refusals, steadfast at first, grew considerably weaker in conviction as the days passed, and Dad's persuasive rhetoric gained momentum. Only one hindrance blocked his design. It didn't matter what he wanted or what I wanted; the cold fact was that Army regulations would not allow me to remain in the service because of my pregnancy. At least I had a respite—until my father thought of another scheme.

I hurried back to Louisiana as quickly as I could, eager to see Mark. Yet instead of my finding him pining away in lonely solitude, I arrived at a trailer filled with a bunch of creeps, including Mark, engaged in a pot party among other attractions. This would not be my last nor worst disappointment.

Soon after my return with the car I received my discharge from the Army. My father was furious and expressed his rage in a blistering letter to me. He exhausted his extensive vocabulary of vile names in referring to me, and charged, among other accusations, that my pregnancy was deliberately planned so I could escape the Army. Many of the insults directed at me and my condition were written in the context of ethnic slurs, which were yet another reflection of my father's detestable character.

I must say that I countered with a peppery letter of my own. The mail route was blue with smoke in both directions. He was thoroughly shaken by the rancorous tone of my reply and hastened to make amends. I don't know if he felt that I was a threat to his security or that he had blown any future chance of recruiting me. Whatever the cause, he soon paid me an unexpected visit.

His greeting was conciliatory, but my reception was both cool and suspicious. My father was so smooth he could talk a cripple out of his crutches, and I soon warmed to his loquaciousness. To my surprise, he skirted the subject of my

Army career and didn't mention the matter of classified
information. This time his overture was as unforeseen as his
visit and was even more incredible than the proposal to steal
military secrets. He guaranteed that it would bring lucrative
dividends.

He began his pitch with a lecture about the inferiority of
all ethnic and racial groups to white Anglos. I had no rebuttal
to what he was saying, nor did I have any idea what he was
leading to. He completely stunned me when he followed this
outpouring of racial prejudice by announcing that he was
active in the Ku Klux Klan. His interest had first been
aroused by the pronouncements of a fellow crew member
from his time of active submarine duty, who, according to
my father, was now a Grand Dragon. He proceeded to list
the stellar virtues of the Klan and decried the public
misunderstanding of the organization. His discourse
culminated in an offer for me to make big money by helping
him recruit people, both old and young, into the KKK.

Most of the rest of the day passed with my listening to
the practiced rhetoric of my father, which was repeated for
Mark's benefit when he got home. Mark's animosity toward
my father the spy was put aside for the moment out of
kinship with my father the bigot. Dad left the next day after
eliciting from us a commitment to give serious consideration
to his proposal. I remember wondering what kind of fortune
he would have made had he been a salesman.

Chris was born on April 13, 1980. That was also the day
when I realized that my marriage was doomed. Mark no
longer tried to conceal the fact that he felt himself to be
trapped in an unwanted marriage and was positively
unwilling to change his feelings. When I went into labor, he
checked me into the hospital, dutifully saw me settled in my
room, and then absented himself with the threadbare excuse
of needing a cigarette. During the next few hours the
physical travail of childbirth was overridden by my emotional
anguish of rejection. I needed the strength of my husband

undergirding me, doubly so since I was informed that my baby's birth would have to be caesarean.

I learned later that on that day Mark applied for and received a one-week leave because I was giving birth. He did not spent those days with me but rather in partying with his friends. Chris and I remained in the hospital for a week. During the whole of that time, Mark visited only twice, staying a few minutes on each occasion. He did not want to hold our baby. One of the visits was for the undisguised purpose of getting a check from me so he could buy marijuana. We only had $70 in our account, and he demanded half of it, not to please me with candy or flowers, not to purchase items needed for a new baby, but to buy drugs for a pot party.

When Mark left with the signed check, I suffered an unbearable emotional assault and began to cry uncontrollably. The kind male nurse who came to attend me did his best to convince me that I was only experiencing common postnatal blues. There was no way I could explain to him the despondency of being rejected by a husband who preferred the company of stoned companions to that of his wife, the kick of smoking a joint to the satisfaction of cuddling his baby.

My homecoming with Chris was rendered joyless by Mark's behavior. The only positive feature of the first few days at home was my rapid physical healing. I could not have managed otherwise. My husband's help was denied me and the baby in every way. His response to the baby's nocturnal cries was to turn over in bed as I painfully got up to feed Chris. Mark didn't changed a single diaper and refused to be bothered by holding Chris. The anguish that had already engulfed me was a mere preview of what was to follow.

I caught Mark in his first lie when he was very late in coming home one night, only a couple of weeks after my release from the hospital. I knew that he had left work at the usual time because earlier I had called his duty station from a neighbor's phone. (We could not afford a telephone of our own because of Mark's expensive drug habit.) Although I had no basis for an accusation, intuitively I knew that he was involved with another woman. Again, although I had no real reason to suspect her, instinctively I felt certain of her identity.

Mark's explanation about his late arrival was that he had pulled extra duty. Even though it was not unexpected, his blatant untruth wounded me grievously. Still I gave no immediate hint of my knowing of his deception, but I determined to ferret out the true facts the next day.

It took little effort to discover my husband's whereabouts the previous night. What I learned from the roommate of the girl I suspected was a stinging slap to my very soul. Mark and one of his cronies had first visited the two girls in their apartment, and then the four of them drove to a lake where they went skinny-dipping. The couples then paired off.

Regardless of a wife's reaction upon discovering her husband's unfaithfulness—injured pride, cold rage, mad jealousy, hysterical grief, fatalistic resignation, trenchant retribution, or whatever—the hurt is the same. As for me, the confirmation of what I had feared seemed to be death itself. Only my love for my baby steeled my resolve to survive.

When I confronted Mark, he was irate, denying that anything improper had take place. "We were just having some innocent fun," he explained. I didn't make an issue of the fact that his concept of innocence was considerably broader than mine. Instead, I harped on the point of his deception. He couldn't deny the lie, so he gave me the finger and stalked off in a huff. If there had been even the slightest suggestion of remorse or apology, my misery would have abated somewhat—but there was none. Mark dismissed me as an overreacting prude and acted as if he were the wronged one.

The breach between us widened. I was tormented by a recurring nightmare of finding Mark with this girl. He would just sneer at me and tell me to mind my own business. Sex between us ceased to be a mystical expression of intimate love; it became instead the brute-level expression of a bodily function, performed with the unfeeling professionalism of a prostitute with her John. The demand was always for me to satisfy him. There was never a concern for my own needs. When I failed to fulfill his expectations, especially when his demands were cruelly selfish or obscenely perverted, he became abusive.

I was completely alone in caring for Chris. He was an adorable baby who captivated everyone who saw him. His own father, however, was altogether indifferent. His inattentiveness expressed itself in many ways, primarily in his refusal to assist me in taking care of the baby at home and in his irresponsibility in such matters as taking us to and from appointments with the doctor. It was embarrassing both to cancel an appointment because of lack of transportation and to wait for hours after an appointment because of Mark's forgetfulness.

My social life was zilch. Even if I had friends, I couldn't visit during the day because Mark always had the car. On the rare occasions that he took me somewhere, the fact that he was invariably drunk or stoned assured an unpleasant evening. If we went to the movies, it had to be at a drive-in so Mark could drink beer and smoke pot. Without fail he would fall asleep in the middle of the picture, leaving me to watch the rest of the movie alone and to deal with the embarrassment of his snores, which could be heard above the theater speakers four cars away. I was infinitely lonely and ardently yearned for a close friend to help bear my burden.

My longing was quickly realized when I met Marie Hammond, who was five years older than my twenty and whose husband was Mark's immediate superior. One day when Chris was five weeks old, he and I accompanied Mark when he drove Bill home. Upon our arrival, Marie came to the car to meet me and to see the baby. Much later she told me that then the Lord spoke these words to her inner understanding: "She is very special to me." Had she told me sooner about receiving such a message, I would have thought her peculiar in claiming that God talked to her and would have dismissed the message itself as patently false, as though God could possibly be interested in someone with a record like mine.

Nevertheless, the supposed communication from the Lord prompted Marie to visit me regularly. In time we were bonded together in a strong friendship. Gaining such a relationship was not without difficulty. My transient background had always prevented my developing an enduring friendship, and my street classes had taught me to distrust anyone but myself. Furthermore, whatever friends I had cultivated were always in my own category, and that didn't lend itself to stable relationships. Marie, however, displayed a transparent sincerity and worked hard to promote our friendship. My distrust of others, confirmed by the deceits of those around me, faded away as Marie made no demands upon me and expected nothing in return for her acts of kindness.

I had never before been acquainted with anyone like her. She had absolutely nothing to gain from befriending me. Marie seemed to care for me for my sake and not her own. She quickly perceived that all was not well with my marriage, an insight that required no special cognitive powers. Although she didn't pry, Marie at first was puzzled by our financial distress. She had seen literally bare cupboards in the trailer and had known me to pin dishtowels on Chris because we couldn't afford diapers. I couldn't tell her that my husband was a druggie who gave scant attention to his family; however, she soon discovered these things on her own.

It soon became apparent that I would have to find a job if we were to survive. I went to work at Howard's Corner Grocery in Leesville. Mark took the car every day, so I walked to work after first walking Chris to the babysitter's house. My hours were from 2:00 to 10:00 P.M., which meant that I had to walk back to get Chris and then walk home in the dark.

It would have been a simple matter for Mark to pick up Chris when he got off work in the late afternoon, thus saving babysitting money and sparing me a longer walk home. For that matter, he could have picked me up from work also, but I didn't suggest it. If he couldn't be bothered to go after his baby, he certainly wouldn't be bothered with me. His inconsiderate selfishness was without limit.

Fortunately, Howard allowed me to take as much of my $75 weekly salary as I wanted in groceries, leaving little to finance Mark's habits. At least we could eat.

Again Marie proved her friendship. She was outraged after learning of my transportation problem. Thereafter she herself came to collect Chris and me each night. This woman was an open Bible to me; I saw its teachings demonstrated in her. I understood very little about spiritual matters and had always thought that being "saved" simply meant a better chance to get to heaven. I knew nothing of a personal relationship with a contemporary Jesus Christ that could affect every part of my life.

Marie used terminology that was completely foreign to me, although it was a natural part of her vocabulary. I had no Bible, so she gave me one along with some helpful Christian literature. I became a human sponge, saturating myself with all I could learn through reading and listening. Marie was never preachy or judgmental in serving as my mentor; she patiently endured my foibles. A transformation was slowly begun in my life. The seed planted five years before at a Baptist church in Norfolk was watered and began to grow.

As my interests turned in a new direction, the gap between my husband and me expanded. Mark himself wanted nothing to do with the Hammonds. Yet he was happy for Chris and me to spend Saturday nights with them and attend church services the next day. It was later that I learned that my absence allowed him to throw parties in the trailer. The most crushing news of all was learning that while Chris and I were visiting the Hammonds on most Saturday evenings, Mark was having sex with other women in our bed.

One hot day in June Mark was at the lake with one of his buddies and two girls and didn't return until three the next morning. He stumbled into the bedroom where I had cried myself to sleep and awakened me with the news that he had been ticketed for driving while intoxicated. He neglected to add that he had wrecked our car. The damage was so extensive that it was two months before the car was repaired.

In July, when Mark decided to continue in the Army, he discovered that his DUI conviction would preclude his reenlistment. Since it appeared that he would leave the Army when his term of enlistment expired and because we were in such financial straits, I accepted my father's offer to come to Virginia where he could help me get a solid job.

Chris and I relocated to Norfolk, where I secured a terrific job with the Honeywell Corporation. Relieved of the strain of coping with Mark's indiscretions and the worry of finances, I was more relaxed than I had been in two years. The only disturbing factor was being forced to endure Dad's constant endeavors to persuade me to reenlist. He insisted that I visit recruiters for the various military branches, which I did merely to placate him. The ploy he used most often in his attempts to get me to sign up again was to lecture me about being a responsible person, especially when I had the opportunity to earn a lot of money.

The KKK involvement was still a viable issue. Dad's disappointment in Mark and me for failing to give thoughtful consideration to his proposal was lessened somewhat when I told him that we rarely considered anything together. He wanted to indoctrinate me into things concerning the Klan, so I agreed to join him in the secret ritual of initiation.

What followed would be ridiculously comical if it weren't so devilishly real and evil. The ceremony featuring my father in his KKK outfit, burning candles, secret oaths and handshakes, as well as other weird rigmarole, had an opposite effect on me than what he desired. The whole affair struck me as being satanic, and I wanted nothing further to do with it.

Barely two months after Chris and I arrived in Virginia, Mark informed me that his superiors, including Bill Hammond, had succeeded in gaining a waiver for him on the DUI conviction. It appeared that he would reenlist after all. I quit my job and made plans to return to Louisiana.

I never thought it possible for my father to feel concern for my welfare, but he seemed to be genuine in his objections to my return. He had sized up Mark when they first met and had perceived that I was going to be badly hurt—just as he had hurt my mother. I marveled that he was capable of feeling even the slightest twinge of compassion.

My return to Louisiana was greeted by ample evidence of my husband's unreliable nature. All the utilities had been disconnected for lack of payment, and the rent had not been paid since I left. I stood holding my five-month-old baby in the heat of the trailer, while Mark, without explanation or apology, sat down, smoked a joint, and glanced at me with a look that said, "Fix it!"

# 7

July 3, 1982
Hayward, California

I learned the meaning of despair in California. I also learned that despondent feelings are most profound in the silence of the still hours which precede the early morning stirrings of a new day. Darkness is allied with loneliness because the colors are the same, and silence deepens distress, unless one uses it as an opportunity to hear the still, small voice of God.

It was well past midnight, and my panic at losing my son had subsided into a dull sensation of emptiness. I had cried until my sobs could no longer be accompanied by tears. For hours I sat in the familiarity of Chris's room, as though touching his things would bring him near to me. I also prayed—desperately—as I never had before. I had traveled a tortuous road from Fort Polk to this point and cursed the treachery of the man who was responsible for the two-year journey.

Mark had not reenlisted in the army after all. Not only had I given up a solid job in Norfolk to return to Louisiana, but we were deeply in debt. My husband had not paid his rent or utility bills while I was away. Mark had instead incurred a debt of almost a thousand dollars to a dope peddler. I lived in constant fear of violence against us in an effort to settle the debt. As usual, however, Mark was unfazed.

To relieve the pressure by escaping his responsibilities, Mark decided that we would move to Maryland after his term of service was over. There we would live with his mother until we recovered financially. I didn't approve at all but had no choice in the matter. The previous year I had been exposed to Mark's lifestyle in his home territory, and I knew that our marriage would be in far greater jeopardy there. Nevertheless, in November 1980 we sneaked out of Leesville in the wee hours of the morning, thus evading bill collectors, landlord, and drug dealers.

The only positive feature about my life in Louisiana that I
left behind was my friendship with Marie Hammond. We had
known each other a scant six months, but to me she was
goodness personified, and what I learned under her tutelage
more than offset the aimless education I received on the
streets. She never preached to me but always provided a
visual presentation of what Christian discipleship really
means. I fervently wanted to live as she did. Our parting was
painful to both of us, but we resolved to keep in touch.

Maryland turned out to be only a stopover for us. During
Thanksgiving Margaret and Michael came from Norfolk, and
my mother, Cynthia, and Cynthia's son, Tommy, joined us
from Maine. It was the first time we had all been together in
four years. During this reunion I decided that my marriage
would be more salvageable in Maine, away from some of
Mark's familiar temptations. When I broached the subject to
him, to my amazement he readily agreed.

We were settled in Skowhegan before Christmas. A long
time afterward, Mark confessed to me that he really hadn't
wanted to move to Maine. How I wish he hadn't!

Birds of a feather . . . misery loves company . . . it
takes one to know one—these and similar bromides aptly
describe the relationship of my husband and my mother.
Both were cut from the same cloth, and they recognized
their commonalities. Quite often they spent a lot of time
celebrating their kinship by getting plastered. Mom further
ingratiated herself to Mark by the servile attitude she had
toward men, which she constantly preached to me amid
Mark's amens.

I was never a women's libber, but neither did I feel myself
to be inferior to a man simply because I was a woman. The
kind of unconditional submission that my mother espoused
was to me a perversion of true submission. I know that the
Bible teaches the leadership role of the husband in marriage
and that the wife is to be submissive to him, but I also knew
that the same passage teaches that the husband is to prove
himself worthy of his wife's submission by loving her as Christ

loved the church, that is, with a willingness to die for her.

Mark wasn't willing to walk across the room for me, much less be crucified on my behalf. In addition, authority is to be exercised in the Lord, and there was nothing godly about most of the demands Mark made on me.

Nor could I submit to an unfaithful husband. The pattern of libertinism that Mark had established earlier continued to characterize his lifestyle. We had not been in Maine two months before the telltale signs surfaced again. One particular episode more than any other finally severed the frayed thread of love that had kept me attached to Mark.

Mark had joined the reserves to supplement our combined incomes, and one weekend each month he would go to a nearby town for drills. On one such occasion, he failed to return in time for dinner at Mom's house. Heavy snow was falling as the hours passed, and still he didn't appear. Frantically, I called the sheriff and the hospital to see if there had been any accidents. Finally, at two in the morning, I called Marie to request her prayers. Even though she prayed with me over the phone then, she seemed strangely unconcerned about Mark's safety. It was much later that I learned the significance of her apathy.

Certain that Mark would at least call unless something drastic had happened, my anxiety continued to mount. I did not sleep all night, and it was time to get ready for work. When I went to the closet to get my clothes, I was puzzled that Mark's "civilian" shoes were gone. Hurriedly rummaging through the hanging clothes to see what else was missing, my growing suspicions were confirmed. Mark's absence had been premeditated. The lump of fear that had been weighing heavily in the pit of my stomach all night melted into a nauseating concoction of rage, contempt, and despair that embittered me against my husband.

If any doubt of betrayal lingered, it was soon dispelled by Mark's homecoming just after daylight. He staggered into the house reeking of alcohol and muttered a lame excuse that he had run out of gas. The fact that he was wearing the civilian

clothes which he had taken with him to the drill gave the lie
to his defense. Confronted with the evidence against him,
Mark confessed to spending the night with a woman.

It was over. My marriage had been a farce practically from
its beginning, and I saw no reason to continue the charade. I
no longer felt any love for Mark and certainly could not trust
him. It was evident that he was not going to change. Before
coming to a conclusion about what course of action to take,
I traveled to California to visit Dori, my friend from my
teenage runaway days. The brief time I spent there settled
the issue for me. I would take Chris and start a fresh life for
us on the West Coast.

Mark was philosophically docile upon my return as I gave
him the reasons for my decision to leave him. He readily
acknowledged his dereliction, with the sole explanation that
he had never really loved me because he had not gotten over
his first wife. The first part I believed, but I questioned the
second, concluding that he treated her the same way he
did me.

I was momentarily taken aback later in the day when Mark
asked me to reconsider leaving. Studying his effort to show
outward contrition, I softened a fraction in my loathing of
him. Maybe that's why I agreed to his next suggestion, a
decision that proved to cost me dearly. Mark knew that I was
planning to drive with Chris to California and stay with
Dori until I was secure in a job and had arranged adequate
housing. "It'll be much easier for you," he assured me, "to
leave Chris here while you go ahead and get settled."

This sudden solicitude by one whose chief concern was
his own gratification should have set off every alarm in my
defense system; however, I couldn't find any hidden motives
in his expressed consideration. Besides, my separation from
Chris would be brief, and he would be in the care of Mom
and Cynthia. Mark had shown no interest in our child before,
and I didn't expect him to change now.

Christopher had just celebrated his first birthday and was
my very life. The love that I had been denied I lavished upon

him, not in material ways, but in the intimate ways of a
mother with her child. He was a happy little boy, and his
laughter was to me a sound more melodious than the music of
any symphony. I especially loved to hold him. Invariably,
every night before I went to bed, I picked him up as he was
sleeping and pressed him close to me as though unbounded
love could flow from heart to heart. I spent hours crooning to
him, praying for him, and crying over him, things I supposed
every ordinary mother does. The very thought of being
denied that time even for a few weeks was unbearable.
Anything beyond a temporary separation would have been
unthinkable.

My father had been doggedly persistent in his overtures to
me, and now, learning of my intent to leave Mark and move
to California, he wired money to speed me on my way.

In June 1981 I began the journey across the country. As I
backed out of the driveway, Mom was still harping about
young mothers abandoning their babies and how she would
never do a thing like that. Her diatribe wasn't intended as
advice, but I wish I had listened anyway.

On the way west I went through Texas and stopped at the
home of Larry and Katie Vick, friends from Fort Polk days.
They lived in Pittsburg, a small town east of Dallas. Katie
accompanied me the rest of the trip in order to spend a brief
vacation in California.

I arrived at my destination on a Sunday afternoon, was
welcomed into Dori's household, and began work on Thursday
as a secretary for Citation Builders. Before the month was
over, I had an apartment furnished with odds and ends
mostly donated by Dori and her mother and supplemented by
a few items I was able to buy. Pleased that I was well ahead
of the timetable I had planned before leaving Maine, I felt
secure enough to send for Chris. His room was ready for him,
furnished exactly as I had envisioned it.

Mark was totally unprepared to receive my call for Chris,
in no way expecting that I could accomplish so much in such
a short while. In turn, I was taken unawares by his response,

which was unequivocally to deny me custody of Chris. I exploded in a hysterical rage, most of it directed at Mark's chicanery, but a sufficient portion reserved for my own naiveté for accepting his lies.

It took two weeks of cries, pleas, and threats before Mark revealed his true motive in keeping Chris from me. I could have my son back on one condition—Mark must be included in the package. In other words, he was holding Chris for ransom and the price was himself. Reluctantly, I agreed to Mark's coming to California. I had no real choice if I wanted to be reunited with my child. As a compromise, he promised to find a place of his own if only he could stay with us until he could get settled. As with all other promises he made to me, this one was hardly worth the effort it took to utter it. I rued the day that I left Chris behind, something I would never have done had I foreseen the consequences.

I pondered the reason for Mark's action while awaiting the arrival of my estranged husband and our son. His own explanation was that he had become inseparably attached both to Chris and me and thus wanted to keep the family together. While plausible enough, it just didn't ring true; it was so out of harmony with Mark's character. There had to be something else.

Several more weeks were to pass before Mark could accumulate enough money for the cross-country trip. They arrived in September, three months almost to the day since I had last held Chris. That night Mark pressured me to have sex with him. I had once loved this man with wild abandonment and would have done anything to please him. Now, however, the thought of a physical relationship with him repelled me. Out of a sense of obligation to him as my husband, I serviced him, and that is an apt description of what took place, considering that I engaged in the act with the passive indifference that an overworked professional must feel with her last client of the evening. It was the last time we had any physical contact.

I wanted Mark out of my apartment and out of my life, but he refused to accept my rejection. Instead he seemed to be obsessed with me. Soon after his arrival I formed a twofold theory concerning his desire to hold on to me. In the first place, getting dumped by me would have been a blow to his cocksure manhood. In the second place, in losing me, Mark would forfeit his security blanket. Some of his junkie friends had confessed to me that he bragged to them about what a good thing he had going in his marriage, even though he didn't love me. As he put it, "She takes good care of me." In other words, I was his meal ticket. While I paid the bills and saw that there was food to eat, he could indulge his irresponsible ways, spending his money on liquor, dope, and women.

True to his nature, Mark wasted no time in finding companions like himself. Weeks turned into months, and he gave no indication of moving out. As usual, I was paying all the bills while he contributed nothing. At Christmas he didn't even buy a gift for his son. His thoughtlessness included me also, but that wasn't unusual; he had never given me a gift, not even on my birthday.

My contempt for the man I married intensified. His dalliances with other women continued, and on the evenings he was home he would sit in front of the television, smoking pot, and drinking beer. He had discovered how to get a viewable picture on the Playboy channel, so he would watch pornographic movies and masturbate while doing so. It was disgusting.

Our financial situation was perilous. Because of past and present loans we were some $10,000 in debt. Our combined incomes since we were married were enough on which to live comfortably under ordinary circumstances, but supporting a drug and alcohol habit is not ordinary. A huge percentage of our income was wasted on Mark's indulgences, and we were in trouble. Convinced that we had no choice, we filed for bankruptcy. The court worked out a sensible plan for us to

pay our debts. At least it would have been sensible if Mark
had fulfilled his part of the plan. As it was to turn out, I soon
found myself saddled with the entire burden.

Mark's detestable nature began to manifest itself in more
violent ways as he physically maltreated me. On several
occasions, especially when he had been drinking, he battered
me around. That kind of abuse was less tormenting than
another kind of aggravation he caused me. He often
threatened to take Chris and go on the run. At first I didn't
think he was serious. He had never exercised a father's
responsibilities or affection toward Chris. I knew his threats
were only meant to upset me, and they succeeded.

Through this difficult time I tried to maintain an active
spiritual life through church attendance and reading the
Bible and helpful books. Still, I felt hypocritical trying to be
a Christian and at the same time desiring to rid myself of my
husband. The conflicting advice well-meaning counselors gave
me added to my confusion. Some people told me that I had
scriptural grounds for divorcing Mark and should do so
immediately lest I become contaminated by him. Others
sought to persuade me to try to preserve the marriage and
win Mark over by my submission to him as my husband. I
delayed doing anything.

I was briefly diverted from marital concerns early in
February 1982. My father called from the home of his
friend, Jerry Whitworth. He was visiting for a few days.
Although I had not seen Dad for almost two years, he
persisted in his efforts to recruit me as a spy. Still I was eager
to see him, but I hoped that the subject of espionage would
not arise. It didn't, at least for the next two evenings which I
spent in the company of my father and the Whitworths. As
far as I was concerned, both evenings were a wash-out with
the three of them trying to one-up each other with their
knowledge of the so-called finer things of life—fine foods,
exotic places, literature, music, and so forth. I was so out of
place, I might as well have been a cat at a dog show.

On the third day of Dad's visit, he took Chris and me to a

park for a picture-taking session. It wasn't long before he revealed the real purpose of his trip. What he had to say stunned me. "My man in Europe is becoming concerned about your age," he tersely announced. I would soon reach twenty-two, and why that ancient age would make anybody jittery was beyond me. Perhaps there was anxiety that I would be too old to reenlist or maybe I would be past the normal age for rookie spies. Whatever Dad's statement about my age meant, I couldn't miss the implication that someone in Europe was advising him about me.

"Who was it, and what does this mean?" "Have I been under surveillance, or am I now being watched?" My questions surely betrayed a pounding heart. The answers were "It's not important" and "No." My father was just full of information. Brushing aside my inquiries, he began to paint an undisguised picture of how I could help him and what I could expect in return. Primarily, he was interested in secret codes and information pertaining to equipment, troop movements, and so on. As compensation I would receive both a regular salary and payment for each piece of information I delivered, depending on its value. Dad then rehashed instructions on covering my wealth, providing illustrations from his own experience. With that, however, I was well acquainted.

An obvious concern was Chris, a subject about which my father had evidently already thought out because he had prepared answers for all my objections. Since single parents cannot enlist in the Army and remain legal guardians of their children, he could be named Chris's guardian and provide a full-time nanny to look after him. If I were stationed overseas, he would see to it that Chris was nearby.

I had only one defense left, which Dad had no way of anticipating. I explained that doing what he was asking would be contrary to Christian principles. He was caught unawares by my sudden confession of being a Christian. At best he managed to express a nebulous belief in the "Almighty," but that didn't interfere with making money.

Dad left that day, still refusing to accept my negative answer as final. Over the next few months he called repeatedly, pressuring me to change my mind. As an act of good faith he sent me money to aid in divorce proceedings against Mark. It was far from sufficient, however, and I never used it for that purpose. I was tempted to take Chris and relocate to Virginia at my father's invitation, but realized I would have no respite from his attempts to enlist me as an agent.

Finally I wrote him a letter that spelled out no in terms that even he could understand. I explained that I had no intention of returning to the Army and had no interest in earning money as a spy. Furthermore, I didn't want to be his partner; I wanted to be his daughter. He called me after receiving the letter, and although he was civil enough, he was obviously upset with me. He finally got the message, he said, and would not badger me any more. I wondered if this meant he would also give up on fatherhood.

On April 22, 1982, my birthday, a Bible study in my apartment was just concluding when Mark called. He was in jail and wanted me to bail him out. He had been parked with a woman when a police patrol stopped to investigate. They discovered an outstanding warrant for his arrest because of an unpaid traffic ticket. I was sorely tempted to leave him where he was. It had been seven long months since he had arrived, and I was weary of his shenanigans. Instead, I paid his fine.

I needed a distraction. To me Mark had become the epitome of abject manhood, and I was fed up with living in the same apartment with him. In addition, all my fruitless prayers came rebounding off the ceiling back to me, mocking me with their emptiness. God was evidently snoozing behind a celestial cloud or else was too engaged with weightier matters to take note of my petty worries. I was feeling my littleness and needed a boost.

The night after I sprang Mark from jail, I went to a disco with Pam, Dori's sister. Dancing always seemed to set me free and left me uninhibited, but on this occasion, the music and laughter were powerless to overcome my empty loneliness. I suppose it's a safe rule not to look for right things in wrong places because you may find an imitation that looks true, but will ultimately prove its falsehood. It was around 2:00 A.M. that I met Steven, and he looked real.

Two weeks later Chris and I moved in with Pam, leaving Mark alone in the apartment. After a few days I borrowed enough money from Jerry Whitworth to pay a deposit on another apartment. Since the time I spent with him and my father in February, I had developed a growing suspicion that he was involved with Dad in espionage activities, but I had no evidence. At any rate, he was most willing to help me.

Even though I was free from Mark, I still had to contend with him. He would sit outside my apartment for hours at a time, watching who was entering and leaving. Steven and I had been seeing each other on a regular basis, and Mark's hostility was especially directed at him. The only way I mollified my offensive husband was to agree to have him over for dinner every Friday night so we could pretend to be a family.

Thus a pattern was established over the next few weeks. I hoped that Mark had ceased his terrorist tactics and would get out of my life, which is exactly what he did on that simmering July day in 1982, but he also took my life with him in the person of my two-year-old baby.

Why did he carry out his threat to take Chris from me? I turned over every conceivable possibility, discarding each in turn until only one remained. He had decided to inflict the cruelest form of punishment upon me that he could possibly devise. There was no worse way for him to drag me through hell.

# 8

July 2, 1983
In the Air between
California and New York

On board the red-eye special to New York, I craned my neck back as far as I could to watch the receding lights of San Francisco, wondering if Steven had remained at the airport to see my plane take off. He told me he would, but there was such an undeniable sense of finality to our parting that perhaps he figured he was long overdue in getting on with his life. So was I. My life had been cruelly snatched away from me on this same date one year before, and I was determined to regain it. I had died exactly 365 times since I had last seen my child, but my resurrection wouldn't be long in coming. If hope turned into reality, I would soon be reunited with Chris.

I reclined my seat and gratefully yielded to my weariness, but the memory of Mark's telephone call at this same hour a year ago evoked too much anguish to allow sleep. He indeed had called as Dave told me he would, but there was no comfort in the brief communication. When I answered, Mark's voice, almost triumphantly vicious in its total lack of sympathy with my plight, bluntly announced: "Chris is with me. He's all right. I'll call again in a couple of days." The only response to my pleas was the click of the receiver as Mark hung up the phone.

He called again after arriving in Maryland, where he and Chris were staying with Mark's parents. Once again he was speaking from a power position, and the vindictive tone of his voice betrayed his callous indifference to my grief. My sobs made complete sentences impossible. Mark wanted me to beg, so I shamelessly groveled to his amusement. It didn't matter to me that I was debasing myself. At that moment I would have promised anything for the return of my child. I desperately tried to pry open any particle of mercy that might be locked away in Mark's soul, but I might as well have

119

been pleading with a block of ice. When I asked why and how he could do such a thing, his answer was an order not to try anything. The command was followed by a threat: "Don't forget that I know your father's secret. If you do anything to get Chris back, your father has had it." His response to my stunned requests for clarification was simply, "I think you understand."

The only redeeming feature about the call was that Mark allowed me to talk to Chris. I was crying so hard he couldn't understand what I was trying to tell him. He kept asking me why I was crying, and the only uncomplicated explanation I could give him was, "Because I miss you so much." Before we said good-bye, his babyish voice spoke words very familiar to me, words I was accustomed to hearing as his last utterance every night: "I love you, Mommy."

It was beyond my capacity to endure, and I cried hysterically. Those words became a treasure to me, and I resolved that somehow, however long it took, I would get back my child. I couldn't stand the thought of his forgetting me, so I prayed fervently that he would dream about me or that something would remind him of me constantly.

I had no legal recourse and no money to pursue that route even if I did have. Mark had lied to me all the time he had been assuring me that he was keeping up his part of the payments on the bankruptcy settlement. He had not, and now it was my responsibility to meet that obligation. I fell heir as well to all the other debts he left unpaid. I consulted the lawyer who had handled the bankruptcy case but received only discouragement. Nothing could be done, and I was liable for the debts.

My father had to be told about Mark's threat, even though I knew he would be implacably angry with me. I had never told him that I had shared with Mark my knowledge of his espionage activities. Thinking that my mother could handle the situation better than me, I first called her. My own despair over the loss of Chris drew no expression of sympathy from her, not even an inquiry about how I was bearing up under the distress, much less words of encouragement to support me. News of Mark's threat, however, provoked an immediate reaction and she agreed to call Dad.

As I expected, he wasted no time in calling me, and his frame of mind was as bad as I anticipated. The mildest statement he uttered was his first: "How could you have told that - - - - - - - - s.o.b. about me?" After that warm-up, his language became as heated as his emotions, filled with expletives and insults. With his rage somewhat vented and his vocabulary depleted to some extent, he offered me advice. Essentially, he demanded that I do nothing that would incite Mark to follow through on his threat. It did not matter at all to my father that my welfare was in jeopardy, and like my mother he expressed no concern.

The insensitivity of my parents added weight to the misery that was already crushing me. My father's attitude toward me I could understand better than my mother's protective manner regarding him. He, of course, would be fearful of exposure, but what did she have to fear? Perhaps she could be charged as an accessory. Or it could be that Michael, who had recently enlisted in the Navy, was her chief concern. How would it affect his career if it became known that his father had sold out his country?

Whatever the explanation, my own situation was of no importance to my parents. Mom even blamed the whole thing on me. Mark would never have left had I been a dutiful wife, and both he and Chris would still be with me. Even now, I had only to to exhibit a humble, repentant attitude, and the rift would be healed. I couldn't help but think, "After her own marital experiences, who was she to moralize at me?"

Dad soon called again, and it was obvious that he had given serious, if misguided, thought to the case. Again he cautioned me to take no action, or as he put it, "Don't dare rock the boat." As if I could rock a boat that was already overturned and sinking rapidly!

He followed his admonition with a string of questions about Mark. "Do you love your husband?" I despise and detest him.

"What do you think of him?" He's a despicable louse. "Would you be sad if something bad happened to him?" I would be totally unconcerned. "What if he were to die suddenly?" Then I would be free of him and have my son again.

I could scarcely believe the underlying suggestion of his questions, but it was nevertheless there. Abruptly he turned to the problem of getting Chris back, reminding me that kidnapping was illegal. I thought his little commentary on the law was ironic on two counts. First, he was talking about my kidnapping Chris, not about Mark's snatching him away from me. In actuality, the law would recognize no crime in either case because custody had not been granted to either of us. Second, it was ludicrous that a person involved in activities like my father was should be qualified to lecture on obedience to the law.

Dad obviously never enacted his unspoken threat to terminate Mark. To be truthful, in my murderous frame of mind, I nurtured the hope that he would do it. When nothing untoward happened, I began to suspect that my father bought Mark's silence. That suspicion was never confirmed.

His second point was an enigma to me. Dad evidently wanted me to renounce any means of regaining my son other than persuasion. Yet he was still lacking in sympathy and offered no support for my cause. I could only surmise that as usual he wanted to exploit the situation in a manner calculated to boost his own interests. Somehow he was trying to bring me under his control, either by a debt of gratitude or by dependence on his guiding wisdom. Whatever the explanation, I resolved that I would chart my own course.

I still hoped that Mark would relent and release Chris to me, and I was puzzled that he had not. After all, he had shown no interest in his child before this time. Furthermore, he had surely discovered that in supporting both Chris and himself he had added obligations, making it more difficult to finance his drug and alcohol dependence. Unfortunately, as the weeks evolved into months, he was still adamant in his refusal to return Chris and kept warning me not to try anything. It soon became apparent that his family was assisting him financially as well as encouraging him in his course of action. Even when they were fully aware of my heart's grief and Mark's depravity, they persisted in their support.

Contributing to my despondency was the fact that I was almost entirely bereft of understanding succor from friends and family. I had few close friends in California, and even they could not comprehend the grief that was eating away at whatever reserve of fortitude I had. They were not cold or heartless, but they lacked the spiritual insight and maturity that would enable them to offer me solid, well-based hope.

Consequently the most that the best of my counselors could extend was an admonition to hang in there, a phrase so empty that it was a mockery to me. Nobody told me where or on what I was supposed to be hanging. I felt myself hanging to be sure, only it was with a noose around my neck. There was no one among my acquaintances who felt qualified to pray fervently for me or with me, and none of them could quote a Scripture passage to instruct or encourage me.

Despite the developing relationship between Steven and me, I was still alone in carrying my burden. He never wanted me to show any emotion when talking about my son, and he became peevish if I burst into tears upon seeing any little boys as old as Chris, as invariably I did.

My financial situation was past the point of desperation. I was responsible not only for my own bills but also for those Mark had left behind, including the bankruptcy settlement. Within days after Chris was taken, I moved from my apartment to a tiny one-room walk-up. There wasn't even a stove in the place, so I prepared my meals on a hot plate. My cheerless surroundings did little to combat the loneliness that engulfed me.

Yet it was in this austere setting that I began to understand the meaning of simple, uncomplicated faith, and how it can prompt equally simple and uncomplicated prayers. I had often prayed, or rather begged, but had never anchored my prayers to anything other than my own desires. No one had ever taught me how to pray in conformity to biblical principles or how to exercise a faith that not only asks but also accepts.

I was certain that God had the ability to come to my aid, but I was less positive about God's willingness. I could find nothing in the Bible that taught anything other than the fact that God loves me and desires the best for me. Slowly I began to understand that faith is not something I should try to conjure up against all odds, but something that rests on what is promised in the Bible.

It also became apparent to me that petitionary prayer should be more than giving God information that He already knows. Basically it must be a confession that my need is beyond my ability to meet it and that I am totally dependent upon God's willingness and readiness to meet my needs.

A turning point of sorts, albeit not in my physical circumstances, came when I prayed like that one night in my comfortless room. As usual, I was crying, but this time instead of whining or begging, I stated positively, "Lord, I know that you can and will restore my son to me"—and I believed what I said. Somehow faith had been given to me, and later I discovered what I had experienced expressed in the Living Bible's paraphrase of Heb. 11:1: "What is faith? It is the confident assurance that something we want is going to happen. It is the certainty that what we hope for is waiting for us, even though we cannot see it up ahead."

That description of faith became something for me to grasp. Sometimes it was a thread so fine as to be invisible, but I still clung to it. Had I foreseen how severely my little faith would be tested, I probably would have loosened my hold rather than go through the hell that I experienced.

The trials, however, had only begun, and severe trials were yet to come. I lost my job, laid off because of a drop in business. During the next few weeks, I went through a succession of jobs, ranging from helping Steven in his sign-making business to working in restaurants and as a secretary. The bank that financed my car swore out a warrant for my arrest. I was late with my payments and had failed to notify them when I moved, so I was charged with evading a creditor.

This little episode was particularly galling because my father could have prevented it. He had cosigned my loan, and the bank had contacted him. Why didn't he give them my new address, which was known to him? More than that, why had he not offered me financial assistance? He was well aware of the difficulties imposed on me, hardships which would be multiplied if I had no transportation to work. By this time I should have become accustomed to the frozen state of my father's compassion, but I still marveled at his cold-heartedness. A more frigid demonstration of his uncaring cruelty was yet to come.

My mother was just as unsympathetic to my cause. She was now demanding that I pay off the loan on Mark's car, which he left in California when he fled with Chris and for which she had cosigned. Her demand was based on what to her was inexorable logic. I was to blame for everything that had transpired. If I had never gone to California in the first place, Mark would not have needed a car, nor would I be without Chris. How long did it take her to reason all that out?

Not long afterwards, I went out to my car one morning to drive to a job I had just started. There was no car! It had been repossessed without prior notification. My father had turned his back on me completely, but he still had one more dart to hurl.

It was Christmas week and Dad was the only member of my family to send me any kind of greeting. His Christmas card turned out to be a handwritten bill on the balance due on the car, including repossession fees. This bit of cheer was to be the last communication I ever received from my father.

Dad's knife in my back wasn't the only reason I had a miserable Christmas in 1982. I had now been separated from Chris for six months and had not cried more profusely than on this traditionally happiest of days. Steven insisted that I spend the day with him and his family, but I might as well have been thousands of miles away—all my thoughts were there anyway. I excused myself early and went to my bleak room, where I sat alone staring into the darkness for hours.

By the time spring arrived, I had deteriorated both emotionally and physically to the point that others were solicitous about my health. Not long after my car was repossessed, I moved once again, this time to a room in a private house. My routine was so unvaried that I might as well have been automated. Robotlike, I left for work early in the morning, came home in the evening, and went to bed around 6:00 P.M., not even bothering to eat. On weekends I rarely left my room, but lay in my bed crying. The woman with whom I lived was kind enough, inquiring often about my welfare, but my predicament was too much for her to handle.

Steven and I drifted apart, and I knew I was at fault. My funereal disposition wasn't highly conducive to merrymaking, and I was always preoccupied with my problems. I had lost so much weight that most people thought I was anorexic. Some of my friends began avoiding me because I had become so edgy that I lashed out at the tiniest irritation. I was transformed into a grumpy crab and seemed powerless to halt the change.

It might seem paradoxical to speak of faith in the face of my depression, but despite my situation I managed a weak grip on that slender thread spun by Heb. 11:1. Throughout the months of dark hopelessness, Marie Hammond had been a beacon keeping me from being totally immersed in blackness. I usually called her during my bleakest times, regardless of the hour, and she never failed to respond with words I needed to hear.

In one way, however, she did not succeed. Ever since Chris's abduction, she tried to persuade me to come and stay with her, but I could see little benefit in such a arrangement and only an imposition to her.

By June I reached my low point. My baby was now three years old. What must he think of his absentee mother who missed his birthday and never came to see him? Everything had crumbled around me, and I felt isolated, tossed about on a sea of loneliness. Marie, anxious about my mental state, renewed her attempts to convince me to leave California and join her. By this time she and her children had left Louisiana for upstate New York, where she was caring for her ailing grandmother while Bill was awaiting transfer to Germany.

She added a strong inducement to the invitation to live with her that further weakened my reluctance. If I came, she would conspire with me to get Chris in such a way that Mark could not possibly stop us. Over the past months I had devised a thousand schemes that promised the return of my son, but I lacked the resources to act on any of them. This, however, was a solid opportunity, and I was tempted.

First, I had to make a final appeal to Mark in an effort to overcome his brutal obstinacy. I had called countless times since he left, trying to break down his resistance and also to talk to Chris. Mark was unyielding, and Chris wondered why I cried harder each time I tried to talk to him.

On this occasion I wasted no time in trying to reason with Mark, but immediately began to beg him with all the shameless groveling I could muster. He was completely unmoved by my pleadings, except to smirk at my abjectness.

There was nothing left to do if I were to survive this nightmare other than to accept Marie's offer. Somehow I scraped together enough money for a one-way plane ticket to New York. I had absolutely nothing to take with me except a few articles of clothing.

Before leaving, I called my mother to share my intentions with her. Rather than encourage me, she tried to divert me. According to her, I would be jeopardizing both Dad's secret and Michael's career. Never mind that in protecting them I would be sacrificing my son. I couldn't let that happen.

I told Steven that I would return to California as soon as I got Chris, but it's doubtful that either one of us really believed it. It sounded so ridiculously simple when Marie and I discussed it. Would it in fact prove to be so?

There is no adequate way I can express the pain that bound me during the first year of my separation from Chris. I have tried, but words printed on paper, while able to describe an image, are lifeless in communicating a feeling that must be experienced before it can be known. That year was a hellish existence for me, and only divine grace enabled me to endure it.

# 9

## August 1983
## South Dayton, New York

I have learned the meaning of Prov. 13:12: "Hope deferred makes the heart sick." I arrived in Buffalo on July 3 spilling over with hope, but disappointment stacked on top of disappointment. Although physically closer, I was further from Chris than when I was in California. At least when I was in California I knew where he was, but now even that knowledge was denied me.

Marie tried unsuccessfully to conceal her astonishment at my appearance when she greeted me at the airport. It had been three years since we last saw one another, and she was stunned by my emaciated state. Halfheartedly I made an effort to cover her embarrassment with a painful witticism that derided my condition, but I only managed to expose the depth of inner grief that I was carrying. The brief silence that followed was far from awkward; instead it was rather pregnant with meaning. Her look of sympathy and her embrace symbolized an understanding with much more eloquence than words.

The changes wrought in me by the severity of an unhappy marriage—compounded by the ruinous events of the past year—were more than physical. I had developed a barbed personality as a defense mechanism against those who I believed would abuse me in any way. I tried to strike first, usually with a curt remark that told the person to whom it was directed that I would not be misused.

I also carried a melancholy air that was terribly reluctant to give way to the freshness of true medicinal gaiety. That characteristic shouldn't be strange; hell has no joy, and I had been there for a year.

I was well aware of both of these negative elements in my disposition, and I wasn't pleased with either one. I needed help in breaking out of my prison and looked to Marie as my

deliverer. She didn't disappoint me. In only minutes she had
diagnosed my condition and began administering the proper
prescription. The therapy began with my surroundings, a
rambling farmhouse situated on several acres of land near
South Dayton, a small town directly south of Buffalo. Marie's
grandmother, a valiant and kindly woman who refused to
yield to the ravages of Lou Gehrig's disease, had lived there
alone since her husband's death a few years earlier. Only
recently had Marie and her two boys arrived to care for her.
Even with my presence there was still plenty of room in the
old comfortable homestead, and I was welcomed as part of
the family.

Marie led me to an enormous upstairs bedroom that
swallowed me and my meager possessions. She found it
difficult to believe that my one medium-sized suitcase carried
all my clothing and other personal items. She wondered when
we could expect the rest. "That's everything I own," I
confessed as I began to cry softly.

It had to come out and now was as good a time as any.
Marie already knew the details of my predicament, except, of
course, the fact that Mark was dangling a sword of Damocles
over my head in the form of my father's secret. I was not
ready to share that peril with her, and there was little other
information I could give her. Mostly I just wept in the
comfort of her understanding presence. Somehow it had a
cleansing, tranquilizing effect on me, and I soon drifted into
an untroubled sleep.

Awakening from my restorative nap, I investigated my new
environment. From the window of my room I could look upon
fields that once must have been productive but were now
overgrown. Still, they seemed to be inviting barefoot
exploration. A small, well-tended vegetable garden was the
only tillage in evidence. There was no livestock, but a few
dogs and several more cats thought they owned the place.

Gramma, as Marie's grandmother was affectionately called,
won me over by her warmth and magnanimous spirit. She
remained active and never sought pity despite the advanced

state of the disease that was suffocating her. I knew that I would receive lots of healing TLC in this household.

That first night Marie and I excitedly conspired over some plans to retrieve Chris. We were more like schoolgirls planning a mischievous lark than two serious adults mapping out a strategy that would alter the lives of several people, including my own. It was such an unimaginative undertaking that I was convinced we could pull it off, amateurs though we were. In no time I was more relaxed than I had been in years, and both Marie and I were laughing, an exercise I had almost forgotten.

Our plan was easily finalized, and I was ready to put it into action immediately. We would drive to Maryland and stake out Mark's house. When he left in the morning we would follow him to the babysitter's house. After he dropped off Chris and went on to work I would straightforwardly march up to the house, take my son, and leave.

There was only one snag, but it was a major one. Money. Marie had the car, but neither of us had the cash that would take us to Maryland and back. We calculated that we needed at least $250. Between us we had about $32.75. Surely, I thought, my mother would help me for such a cause. After all, I had always loaned her money when she asked for it and had never before sought help from her. I was confident of her support and determined to call her the next day.

It was July 4, and soon I would have ample reason to celebrate. How soon hinged on a phone call to Maine. Yet Mom's reaction to my being in New York and my scheme to recover Chris was considerably less than enthusiastic. She was still preaching protectionism of my father's secret activities and Michael's navy career. She showed real emotion, however, when I asked if I could borrow some money from her. In fact, the telephone connection increased in temperature as her voice increased in volume. As best as I could understand it, the gist of her first tirade was, "Where do you think I'm going to get money to send to you?" Actually, what she said was substantially more colorful than that, garnished as it was with some choice adjectives and adverbs modifying some equally descriptive nouns and verbs, with a few free-standing bywords thrown in for emphasis.

When I reminded her with gentle restrain that she had never refused Margaret when she asked for money, and that my need was just as legitimate as any that had prompted my sister's pleas, she delivered another impassioned oration. This one was more personal, aimed directly at me, and she omitted no acrimonious obscenity in dressing me down. Her sign-off just before she slammed the receiver down was a demand that I find somebody else to use.

I was by no means shocked by my mother's vile harangue, having heard similar outpourings since my childhood. I was desperate enough, however, to call her back a few moments later. The line was busy, so I reckoned that she had taken the phone off the hook. I was terribly wrong in my conclusion but didn't know it until four years later. Meanwhile, I considered all ties between my mother and me severed, and resolved not to call her again. I faithfully kept that resolution for almost a year and a half, during which time there was no communication of any kind between us.

The actions of both my parents effectively orphaned me from them. Both had denied me support of any sort, not only financial but also sympathetic encouragement. I had more difficulty trying to analyze my mother's failure to rally to my cause. As a mother she surely had to know what I was going through, but she seemed to be heartlessly and inexplicably untouched by my suffering, an attitude that I could in no way comprehend.

My father's refusal to come to my aid was easily explained. His self-centeredness would not allow him to raise a hand to help anybody, not even his own daughter, particularly if he derived no benefit from it. As long as there was a possibility that I would join him in espionage activities, he did me all kinds of favors, but when that possibility was no longer viable, he lost all benevolent interest in me. He had all the necessary resources to help me. After all, he had been a private investigator since his retirement from the Navy. He had money, connections, and expertise. He only lived two hundred miles from Mark and Chris, and he had a private plane. Additionally, he had been honored for helping parents in being reunited with their abducted children. In my case, however, he lacked a motive for helping me. For that matter, he had a strong motivation to see that I did nothing to upset Mark. The sword of Damocles still swayed.

It was a blessing that I misinterpreted the busy signal when I tried to call my mother again. The phone was not off the hook, but very much in use in a conversation that would do me irreparable harm. Had I known that as the result of that conversation, reunion with my son would be delayed another two years, I would have gone berserk. There is absolutely no way I would have survived had I known that I faced two years of wretchedness far more hellish than the previous year's experiences that I had just endured, and just barely survived at that. Certainly I would have been shattered had I known that my own mother was primarily responsible for these forthcoming two years of despair.

Immediately after slamming the receiver down, terminating my call to her, my mother placed a call to Mark. Perhaps if she had waited for her hot anger to cool, she would not have done so. Nevertheless, either out of spite toward me or a protective attitude toward her former husband and her son, she committed high treason against me by maliciously informing Mark that I was in New York and intended to "kidnap" Chris. That warning was enough for him, and he immediately fled into hiding with Chris. Had I gone to Maryland, I would not have found them.

At the time, however, Marie and I were ignorant of Mom's call to Mark and his subsequent change of address, so we pursued our original course of action. Obviously we had to find another sponsor for our venture. Marie was an avid viewer of the Christian Broadcasting Network's "700 Club" and was familiar with Operation Blessing, the benevolence arm of the ministry. If they gave money to poverty-stricken

people, then we were eminently qualified for aid, but I
wondered if they would finance the kind of project we had
in mind.

I was desperate enough to grasp at any straw, however
fragile it might appear, so with Marie's help I called the
office of Operation Blessing in Virginia Beach, Virginia. The
lady who answered was kind enough to listen to my story but
could offer nothing more than a promise to call me later
when a decision was reached. We felt certain that the only
barrier preventing us from recovering Chris would soon be
removed, so we rehearsed our plan.

Days dragged by and no call came. Finally Marie called
Operation Blessing again. This time we still didn't get
financial help, but at least we got more than a promise. We
got a prayer . . . in tongues . . . without interpretation. I
supposed that procedure was all right since the tongues were
addressed to God and not to us. Actually I didn't know
enough about it to formulate an opinion.

Once again we waited for a decision to be made on our
request for aid. The delay was particularly difficult for me
because my funds were almost depleted, and my
two-pack-a-day cigarette habit was expensive. My brief
divorce from nicotine ended as soon as Chris was born, and
I foolishly resumed the habit that had held me captive since I
was a child. Marie had full sympathy with me in some things
but was pitiless in others, and smoking fit into the latter
category. She thought I was giving the devil a burnt offering
every time I lit up and referred to my little idols as "cancer
sticks." She also parodied the commercial by talking about
walking a mile for a camel and smelling like one when you
get it. Anyway, she relented and contributed to my
delinquency when she realized that I had enough problems
to wreck my nerves without adding a cold turkey to the pot.

More days limped past without a call from the ministry in
Virginia, so an impatient Marie called them once again. I
awakened from a nap and came downstairs to find her
conversing on the phone. Only moments passed before I

realized who was on the other end. Then as Marie grew silent I perceived that the other person was praying. In response to Marie's direction, I picked up the extension to listen. I was just in time to hear the lady praying for the restoration of my marriage—that was too much for me. Obviously she didn't know anything about my marriage, otherwise she wouldn't dream of praying me back into it.

I replaced the phone and walked back into the room where Marie was. Suddenly, she grabbed a pen and began to write furiously. After the call was concluded and I saw what had been written, I questioned her concerning how much information about me she had shared with the lady. She assured me that she had told very little of my general situation and less of the specific details. The woman, she explained, had prayed in tongues and then began speaking words of knowledge, words of wisdom and prophecy, all of which were gifts of the Holy Spirit. I was vaguely familiar with the terms, since they are listed in 1 Corinthians 12, but knew nothing about their actual operation.

The lady on the phone, supposedly speaking as the Spirit directed, had said these words as a preamble to what followed: "I am the Lord your God. Is there anything impossible for me? You have hardened you heart against me." The last statement arrested my attention immediately since I figured that no one but God could have known my actual spiritual condition. I had indeed caught myself entertaining harsh thoughts about God, blaming Him for neglecting me. At the same time, however, I felt God's love and knew that I was experiencing the discipline described in Hebrews 12, which assures us that God loves His children and disciplines them, not for a wanton or destructive purpose, but with a beneficial goal in mind, specifically that of bringing us into his holiness. I must have been a long way from where I should have been because it seemed to me the Lord had been administering extra licks to me.

Still I found it difficult to accept the reality of what had just been spoken over the telephone since it was completely unlike anything I had ever experienced. I tried to discard it as nothing more than the typical Pentecostal manner of doing weird things, but the thread of faith to which I had been clinging pulled me tighter, and I accepted the reality of what Marie had written. People may think I'm crazy for doing so or may dismiss my belief as the natural reaction of a desperate person who will grasp at anything that looks promising, but to this day I stand by my choice and nothing has happened to dislodge me. In fact, subsequent events proved the correctness of my stance.

Marie had scribbled eight items that came forth from the counselor's prophecy. I read them aloud:

1. You are not to return to California to Steven. (How did she know about him, even his name? Marie insisted that she did not reveal it.)
2. Your name is written in the Book of Life. Seal it with water baptism. I desire to give you my Holy Spirit.
3. Learn to give tithes and offerings.
4. Pray for Mark every day.
5. I will return your son to you.
6. The head of your household will be a godly man, and you will have other children.
7. I have a great work for you.
8. Your trials and tribulations are not over yet.

I felt I could handle most of those items, even if number four would be with little enthusiasm and expectation, but the Lord would have to dispense an extra dosage of grace if I were to endure number 8. Some of the statements came to pass quickly.

Only a couple of days had elapsed when a young woman came to the farm bearing a message for me. She had felt strongly impressed by God, she said, that I was to meet a certain pastor in Jamestown, about forty-five minutes to the south. I followed her instructions; Marie took me to his house for a visit. It soon became evident that the Lord hadn't prepared him for a case like mine. He didn't have a clue about what to do after hearing my story. The trip was not in vain, however, since he agreed to baptize me by immersion. The ceremony was duly conducted in the swimming pool of one of his parishioners. It had special significance to me, not only because I knew I was obeying a divine command, but because I received assurance that I was a new creation.

The pastor read some Scriptures and explained that although the Holy Spirit had taken up residence in me from the moment of my conversion, I still needed his fullness, or, as he pointed out from the Bible, to be "baptized in the Holy Spirit." So on the next Sunday we were in attendance at the church where this man was pastor. I had already prayed to be baptized in the Spirit, so went forward in an expectant state when the altar call was given. No one had coached me, so I was uncertain about what would happen but was unprepared for what did occur when the pastor's wife placed her hands on me and began to pray. As soon as her hands touched me, I felt an indescribable power, something like liquid electricity, flow through me. I opened my mouth to speak and words of a language unknown to me flowed forth. I was experiencing a personal Pentecost.

It soon became painfully apparent that we would not be able to go after Chris until later than we hoped, so I had to find a job. The pastor of the church in Jamestown, which we attended for three consecutive Sundays, offered assistance in helping me find work in that city. I could housesit for some of the church members who were going to be away for a week, and he would take me around to different businesses. I wasn't too keen about the idea but agreed to the plan after a stern lecture from Marie.

The week was a mountainous fiasco. I saw the pastor once; some three days later he brought a typewriter for me to type my résumé. I saw only one other person, a church member who spent one hour driving me around to find employment.

The rest of the time no one called or checked to see if I had food. As a matter of fact, I caught up on fasting that week because the food supply soon exhausted and I had no money with which to buy more. The pastor drove me back to the farm very late after the church service on Sunday night. He offered no explanation for the lack of attention given to me during the week.

I wanted to forget the whole thing, but Marie was too upset to let the matter rest. The next day she called the pastor and demanded an explanation. So he told her that it would be a wasted effort for me to look for work, because God would never prosper me as long as I was in rebellion by refusing to submit to my husband. He actually believed that he would be abetting my sin if he helped me in any way to remain separated from Mark. He further stated that God would never restore my son to me since I was the guilty party. In closing his free sermon, he offered Marie a choice piece of advice. She should kick me out so I would be forced to return to Mark. Thus Marie was sinning by providing a sanctuary for me! When she told the pastor that I didn't have a cent of my own, he admonished her to send me to the local YWCA.

I shouldn't have been set back on my heels by this counsel because there were forewarnings of it. Many people were aware of my marital situation and assured me of their prayers on my behalf. Most of them told me that if I earnestly asked God to restore my marriage, He would enable me to love my husband again. That might be okay, but what about his loving me? It seemed to me that one-sided love was the problem in the first place. I did try, however, to pray that way but had to be honest with God and confess my hypocritical feelings in trying to pray for something I didn't really want.

Other counselors went further, telling me that I should take the initiative to return to my husband. Then God, because of my obedience, would grant me love for Mark. No matter what happened, I was supposed to be submissive to him. I think God knew me well enough to perceive that I would rather die than return to the kind of life I had with Mark.

Maybe they were right and I was wrong in my attitude. I was only a novice Christian and could never be mistaken for a Bible exegete, but I determined that I had better be certain about the submission business. Everybody had been quoting Eph. 5:22 to me, so I started there.

There is nothing that I could see in that verse or in the surrounding ones which demands that wives render unconditional obedience to their husbands. In fact, it appeared to me that more emphasis is placed on the husband's obligations to the wife than the other way around. He has been placed in a leadership role, delegated with authority by God, to assure order and tranquility in the home and in society, and his function is not to make imperious demands upon his wife for self-gratification; rather, it is to care for her with a love like that which took Christ to the cross and with the same regard he has for his own body.

Now I could get excited about submitting myself to a husband who loved me like that! If he were truly fulfilling his God-appointed role, then he would put my interests above his own and would see to my every need.

The principle was clear to me because there is a little rider placed on the command for the wife to be subject to the husband. It stipulates that the submission is to be "as unto the Lord." The submission enjoined is really to God's authority, administered by a faithful godly husband who commands only what God commands and forbids only what God forbids. So if the husband misuses or abuses that authority, exploiting it for his own self-interest so that obedience to him would mean disobedience to God, then there is no choice at all. The wife must obey God.

Where did that leave me in relation to Mark? If he loved me as he loved his own body, then he would be deliriously in love with me. As it was, I saw nothing in Ephesians or elsewhere in the Bible that told me I had to be subject to a man like my husband.

There was another matter my counselors overlooked. Again and again the Bible warns against adultery and cites it as grounds for divorce, as in Matt. 19:9. Mark had been unfaithful to me from the very beginning of our relationship. I knew of many instances other than those I have described in which he had sexual intercourse with other women. Even Marie and her husband knew firsthand of some of Mark's sexual liaisons. What she told me at this time stunned me, not because of Mark's infidelity, but because they withheld the information from me.

Marie revealed to me that at Fort Polk, Mark had described me to her husband, Bill, and to others as a shrewish nag who constantly fought with him. As Mark's supervisor, Bill could and often did give him time off in order to attend to his marital problems. Yet when Bill became better acquainted with me, he couldn't picture me in the image that Mark had described. So on one of the occasions when Mark left early, Bill followed him—straight to a tryst with the wife of another soldier. Another time Bill caught Mark having sex with a girl in the back of a truck.

Why did they never tell me these things? What about the husbands of the women with whom Mark was involved? Why did Bill never confront Mark? The answer to all of these questions was a terse, "It was none of our business." I disagreed, but it was too late now.

At any rate, my counselors were giving me terrible advice, even if they felt they were being led by the Lord. Fortunately, God knew me better than they did. So did Marie, who assured me that she would support me in whatever decision I made.

I found a job. Mae's Doughnuts was a twelve-table, eight-seat-counter restaurant located in Silver Creek, twenty minutes from South Dayton. I became the newest waitress there. Once again I was indebted to Marie, who not only provided me with daily transportation but also purchased my uniform and shoes.

The owner of the place was Sam (Mae was his wife), and he fit perfectly the stereotype of the pot-bellied, dirty-aproned, foul-talking small café owner. He was one of the rudest, crudest, and most vulgar men I've ever known. In addition to his vileness as a person, he was terribly unfair as an employer, requiring each waitress to work her shift alone.

Each one of us wound up doing the work of at least two people, taking orders, serving meals, cleaning tables, making coffee, tending the register, boxing donuts, sweeping the floors, and washing dishes. In addition, I had to cook for two hours each day. Sam was particularly harsh with me, mainly because I professed to be a Christian. He never let an opportunity pass to vex me.

In spite of my obnoxious employer, I did well. The customers appreciated my service, and I received generous tips. One man in particular took a personal interest in me, not in an improper way, but in a kind fatherly way. He knew something of my financial difficulties and of Marie's faithfulness in transporting me to and from work.

One day, he dumbfounded me by presenting me a check for $1,800 for the express purpose of buying a car. He made it clear that the gift had no strings whatever attached to it and that I was to feel no obligation to him. I was beginning to learn a lesson about God's provision and His use of individuals as instruments. I converted the money given to me into a Toyota pickup.

Marie and I had our differences, but we had grown extremely close. We were more like sisters than friends. One evening we were engaged in one of our typical conversations that went on for hours. There were still many things about me and my problems that puzzled her. So on this particular night, I gave her the complete picture, including my father's secret and Mark's threat to use it against me. She did not say a word in response but sat there staring at me with a look of astonishment mingled with incredulity.

# 10

Saturday, November 17, 1984
Buffalo, New York

I discovered that loneliness belies the strength of independence. Murphy's law had always been a major factor in my irregular existence, but never more so than in the previous year and a half. I lived like a wreck about to happen, and it usually did. Thanksgiving was only days away, and only seconds would be required for me to take inventory of my stockpile of blessings.

I had arrived in New York the previous year full of optimism that my son and I would soon be reunited and that we would proceed to live in undisturbed contentment. The realization of that joy had been postponed indefinitely as I struggled daily merely to subsist.

Aside from my disappointment at not being able to recover Chris immediately, things continued well enough. I was settled into the routine of life in a vintage farmhouse with friends who had taken me in, and I was resolutely bearing the gibes and deviousness of my villainous employer at Mae's. Marie and I had found a small church in the nearby town of Cherry Creek, and we attended faithfully. I felt myself growing spiritually through the teaching I received at church and through my own prayers and Bible study. By God's grace I had even quit smoking, a habit that had enslaved me for more than ten years. There was no pressure from Marie or anyone else to give it up. It was a simple decision on my part based on a growing conviction that smoking was both harmful to me and dishonoring to Christ. I pictured myself offering Him a cigarette and felt very uncomfortable at the incongruity of such a thing. Every day Marie and I had a lengthy prayer session together in which we boldly presented our petitions to heaven. So on one occasion we simply asked God to help me quit smoking, and in faith I shredded my remaining cigarettes and sacrificed them to the wind. I have not smoked since.

147

California was rarely in my thoughts, and I didn't missed it
at all, except for Steven. He had called soon after my arrival
in New York and confessed that our separation had made
him realize just how much he cared for me. It was too late.
Prophecy or not, I could not return to California. Not without
Chris. In truth, I could not deny a fervent desire to go back
to the man I felt I loved, and my tears were unrestrained as I
tried to explain why I couldn't.

I began to write long letters to Steven, sharing with him
about my new life. At the same time I was certain that he
would be turned off by my witness, supposing me to have
become some kind of religious recluse. It took a while, but he
did respond. Probably it would have been better for me had
he not called, because once again I melted in hot tears as he
expressed both his love for me and his regret at not
appreciating me and for using me only as a convenience.

I began to have vivid and strange dreams, mostly about
Chris. Not a night had passed since he was taken from me
that I failed to go to bed thinking about him, often crying
myself to sleep. So it was more unusual when I didn't dream
about him than when I did, but now the dreams were more
intense and terrifying. They were all different but carried the
same theme of getting close to Chris, yet not near enough to
reach him. Sometimes I would be searching for him in an
enormous house with dozens of rooms. I knew that he was
somewhere in the house but could never find him. In some
dreams I would meet people who had seen him only minutes
before I arrived, and I was always too late. At other times I
would see him in the distance, only to discover after running
to him that it was not Chris at all. Always I awoke crying his
name.

It wasn't long before my dreams took on a shocking reality
after I learned of Mark's fleeing with Chris to a place
unknown to me. I had made no attempt to contact them after
my arrival in New York, fearful that Mark might react exactly
as he did if he learned of my plans. I didn't know at that
time, of course, that my mother had informed him of my

whereabouts and of my intent to come for Chris. Marie and I decided that it would be safe for her to call Mark and inquire as a friend about Chris's welfare. It was then that we found out that he had gone into hiding.

The weeks of summer passed swiftly with only a baffling and disquieting mystery, the Case of the Cornfield Culprits, to serve as a diversion. Marie's grandmother repeatedly insisted that she often saw someone on the hill in the fields beyond the house. We discounted these reports at first as the illusions of an elderly woman whose health was deteriorating, but then both Marie and I began to hear noises from trespassers almost every night.

The noises were specifically directed at me one hot night when I went down into the kitchen to make some tea, wearing only my baby doll pajamas. Only moments after I flipped on the lights, the fields beyond the house resounded with the whistles and delighted shrieks of peepers watching a free burlesque show. The sheriff's office always responded to our urgent calls, albeit with flagging vigor as the pleas became more frequent. They found nothing to suggest that intruders were on the prowl and dismissed us as nervous nellies jumping at sounds made by nocturnal animals.

If the authorities didn't take us seriously, we would take action ourselves. Loaded with cans and string, I marched into the cornfield behind the house and rigged a primitive alarm system at strategic points. When the cans rattled, we would be alerted to the intruder's presence. We didn't have to wait long. Only two nights later the alarm was triggered, followed immediately by a voice. Reluctantly the sheriff dispatched deputies in response to our frantic call, but the trespasser evidently decided not to wait around for them. When one of the deputies sarcastically suggested that a deer clanked the cans, Marie, her voice dripping with honey, answered with the rejoinder that we could make a fortune if we could catch a deer that cussed as fluently as this one did.

More drastic action had to be taken. Thus far we had not been harmed, and nothing had been stolen except some corn, but we felt justified in being frightened. After all, we were two women alone in an isolated farmhouse with two small boys and a helpless old lady. Marie found our "equalizer" in the form of her grandfather's ancient double-barreled shotgun, which was immediately given a place of honor by the window in her bedroom. My CASWAT (Pentagonese for Can Alarm System to Warn Against Trespassers, a hangover from my army days) was still in place. Now we waited expectantly, almost hopefully.

Our opportunity came the very next night when the sounds of interlopers reached us from the nearby field. We had already decided that I would fire the gun, pointing it toward the sky so as not to hit anybody. Our rehearsal earlier that day revealed some imperfections in our scheme that we had to correct. It was impossible for only one of us to hold the heavy weapon in order to fire it. Perhaps both of us could lift it, one grasping the stock to fire it and the other raising the barrel. This plan presented another problem, however. The gun had a kick worse than that of an enraged mule. We figured that whoever fired it would need the bracing support of the other behind her. Not to worry—we could rest the barrel of the gun on the window sill while the two of us got behind the stock to absorb the reaction to the firing. Only a slight adaptation was needed and all would be ready.

The window sill was so low that we had to kneel to rest the barrel of the shotgun on it. So I knelt with the butt of the gun firmly against a pillow held in place at my shoulder by Marie, who knelt in readiness behind me to guard against the likelihood that my shoulder would be dislocated. Bravely I closed my eyes and squeezed the trigger. There was a thunderous roar as both Marie and I were sent flying back halfway across the room. I picked myself up from my sprawled position on the floor and turned to look at Marie. She was saying something to me but no sound came from her mouth, at least that I could hear. Her lips seemed to be asking me if I was okay. I was, except the next day Sam scolded me for serving meals with only one arm—my left one at that.

We enjoyed a couple of peaceful nights, but then CASWAT alerted us again. This time it was Marie's turn to shoot. We had made some modifications in our firing system, which mostly involved moving the bed in order to brace ourselves against it, so it wasn't quite as bad. The kick was just as powerful, though, so Marie got a liniment treatment for her shoulder. This scenario was repeated over the course of many nights, with the two of us alternating at firing the cannon. The trespassers, after their initial fright, must have surmised that we weren't shooting at them and probably enjoyed the fireworks.

We were at a loss to explain the nightly tromps across the fields, and the mystery remained unsolved until the first heavy frost when the traffic ceased. An astute deputy had a theory that proved to be correct. All along, someone had been cultivating and then harvesting a plot of marijuana on a remote section of the farm's property. By the time the deputy found the site, the crop had been reaped and the "produce" taken to "market."

Yet something far more sinister grew out of the cornfield caper. The nearest neighbor, one of those public-spirited souls who minded not only her own business but everybody else's as well, informed Marie's Uncle Elbert about trouble on the farm, embellishing the tale somewhat to make it appear that we were terribly mistreating his mother. My first look at him when he arrived unexpectedly to investigate told me we were in trouble. If my father was the champion of selfish, greedy, uncaring knaves, then this man was runner-up. He may not have invented meanness, but I'd wager he held a few patents on ways to exercise it. Something connected with his research, no doubt. He was a wealthy neurosurgeon in the Buffalo area and yet was so cheap that he refused to see that his mother received adequate care. She was fading rapidly and needed to be institutionalized, or at least be provided with the care of a full-time nurse.

Uncle Elbert, supposedly a respectable family man, had other faults as well, and if his actions toward me were typical,

then his flaws were major. In short, he was a lecherous
philanderer, and wasted no time in coming on to me. After
that first visit to the farm he found reasons to make frequent
trips "to check on things," without his wife. The man had
children older than me, and here he was making advances
toward me. The critical point came on New Year's Eve, which
the doctor spent at the farm. If he thought I would be in a
little more receptive mood to his amorous ways on such a
festive occasion, he was mistaken. He did indeed spend the
night in my bed, but I was safely locked away elsewhere in
the house. If it hadn't been so cold the next morning, he
would have been sweating poison, and I figured retribution
would be forthcoming.

It was. Gramma was steadily declining. She was still
physically strong, but she was mentally and emotionally
unstable. She was prone to wander alone out in the January
cold. For her own protection we were forced at times to lock
her in her room, even to the extent of nailing the windows
shut. We kept Uncle Elbert well informed of her worsening
condition and of the drastic actions we sometimes had to take,
but he completely ignored the situation.

The climax came one day early in February when Marie was
away and I had responsibility for Gramma and Marie's two
young sons. Hearing a commotion in the kitchen, I rushed in
to find Gramma with a heavy pot in her hand about to attack
Jonathan, the older of the two boys. When I intervened, she
turned on me. Finally I calmed her down enough to lead her
to her room, where I promptly locked her in. She was out the
window before I got back to the living room. Thoroughly
exasperated, I called Marie for instructions. "Pacify her
with the promise of taking her visiting, and nail the doors
and window shut," were her directions. I did exactly as she
said.

This done, I relaxed, but almost immediately decided it was
time to go visiting when I saw Gramma heading for the
windows with a claw hammer in her hand. So off we went to
see Milton, an elderly friend of the family who lived down

the road. Unknown to me, while we were there Gramma called Sister Nosy Know-It-All and communicated to her how she was being held prisoner in her own house. Naturally Miss Busybody couldn't wait to inform Uncle Elbert of how his mother was being severely mistreated, adding her own misleading and embellished interpretation to the report.

Sure enough, the baron and his whole clan showed up the next weekend for a family conclave. Never before had I felt such an air of self-assumed authority emanating from an individual who at the same time condescended, as lord of the manor, to deal with inferior beings.

The first dart was hurled at me. "Did you nail the doors and windows shut?" he righteously demanded of me. When I responded with an unqualified yes, he preached a sermon of judgment to me, culminating in my excommunication. He graciously allowed me three days to vacate the premises. Actually I shouldn't have been surprised, having been forewarned of this very thing in a dream several weeks before.

Uncle Elbert's display of heartlessness I could handle, because it was in complete harmony with his mean-spirited disposition. What crushed me was Marie's failure to come to my defense. I stared at her, expecting her to speak a word on my behalf, especially since I was only carrying out her directions regarding her grandmother. She knew I had no place to go and was unemployed, having recently left Mae's because of Sam's humiliating abuse in front of the customers and the promise of another job that failed to materialize. Yet Marie avoided my eyes and remained silent. Her abandonment of me was devastating. It was at her insistence that I was here, and now I was more alone than ever in the quest to find my son. I had just spent the second Christmas away from him and had no idea where he was.

Marie was the next object of Uncle Elbert's displeasure. She had power of attorney to handle her grandmother's affairs, but, legally or not, he declared it void and proceeded to evict her and the boys. He further arranged a $1,000 settlement with her, on the condition that she not contest

Gramma's will. So, although she had as much right of
inheritance as he did, she was left with a bus token while
he drove off with the bus. He had style, that one. Too bad
he couldn't have been a carpetbagger during Reconstruction
days. He would have made a vulture's fortune.

At least Marie had close friends she could stay with, a
monthly income, and a husband who would be sending for her.
I had nothing except my pickup, a few articles of clothing, and
a hundred dollars Marie gave me as conscience money. It was
February, snow drifts were two feet deep, and I was totally
without support. Where could I go? I had no friends and no
job, and the money from Marie would last only so far.

In desperation, I called Joe, a former customer at Mae's.
He had been helpful in the past, offering friendly advice
concerning car problems, tips on shopping, and similar
subjects. I had to be careful, because although Joe was
married, he had always engaged in flirtatious bantering with
me in the manner of some men, and I had no desire to
encourage him in the wrong way. Desperation will drive a
woman a long way, but I hadn't yet got that far.

Guarding my language lest he read into my plea a promise
that wasn't there, I called Joe and explained my plight. He
seemed eager to help and took me to a friend of his who
owned a cheap hotel near Fredonia. There we arranged for a
free room until I could get a job and recover somewhat
financially. I called Marie to inform her of my whereabouts,
but she seemed too preoccupied with her own problems to
be bothered with mine. The sudden reversal in her attitude
both puzzled and grieved me.

A month passed and I was no nearer to employment than
before, although I had scoured every town for miles around
looking for work. Joe's friend was showing signs of wanting to
be rid of his nonpaying guest, while Joe himself was showing
signs of another kind. When he made it unmistakably clear
that I would receive no further help unless I returned the
favors, I left. I still wasn't that desperate.

I lived in my truck, parking it in various places. My few

belongings were stashed in the canopied bed of the pickup, and I slept in the cab where I could keep warm. Finally I accepted an invitation from Diane, another former customer at Mae's, to stay with her. Before recently converting to Christianity, she had been heavily involved in witchcraft and other occultic practices. Unfortunately she had not entirely divorced herself from such things, and weird phenomena still took place in her house. I had always been prone to dream, as I described, but now my dreams took on new dimensions. I was tormented in my sleep, always struggling against evil spirits attempting to take control of me. Many times I awakened during the night shouting the name of Jesus or praying in tongues. Sometimes it seemed that the combat lasted all night, so that in the morning I was more exhausted than when I went to bed. I never mentioned these things to anybody, fearing they would think strange things about me.

During this time my one-hundred-dollar stake, which I had hoarded more jealously than a miser, had dwindled to twenty-five cents. Since it came from Marie in the first place, I decided to return it to her in the form of a telephone call, which just happened to carry a twenty-five-cent toll. It had been almost two months since we last conversed, and once again she seemed untouched by my predicament, preferring her own interests to mine. The climactic slap came when the operator came on the line asking for the deposit of another quarter. When I told Marie I didn't have another coin, instead of telling me to call back collect, she simply signed off with a noncommittal "Talk to you later."

Even the rejection by my parents had not stung like being shunned by my friend. In frustration I wrote Marie a letter, holding back none of the disappointment I felt. The mailing of that letter, for which I had to borrow a stamp, was the lancing of an ugly boil, necessary for the healing process to begin. Within days after receiving the letter, Marie managed to call me, miraculously finding me at a diner that I frequented. Although she was powerless to help me, at least we found reconciliation.

Diane freaked out on me, exploding for no reason. She was unstable to say the least and two weeks of the heavy atmosphere in her house was all I could take. As I drove off after the nasty scene, I was struck by the contradiction of the day. The date was April 22, my birthday and Easter Sunday—a twofold joy, but I did not feel like rejoicing.

I was living in my truck again and wasn't liking it a little bit. An offer of help came from Bob, an acquaintance of Diane who knew the mess I was in. Basically I still considered the pickup as my home but began to use Bob's apartment as a place to eat and bathe and sometimes sleep. Finally, when he moved into a two-bedroom apartment in Fredonia, I moved in with him, but not before making it abundantly clear that there could be no intimate relationship between us. His acceptance of this arrangement didn't deter a jealousy and possessiveness he developed for me. At times his behavior was such that I feared not only for my own life but for the life of any man who dared to show me any attention in public. He kept pressuring me to reward his kindness by dispensing physical favors, but when I refused and threatened to leave, he always relented, even if it was in a petulant manner.

My living situation was made even more bizarre by the fact that Bob was heavily involved in the occult. His mother was a practicing witch who exercised a tremendous influence over him. He himself spent most of his time playing Dungeons and Dragons and similar games with occultic themes. Sometimes a game would go on for days at a time, with the players giving themselves over to it with an obsession that hardly allowed time for eating and sleeping. I persisted in my warnings to Bob about his involvement in such practices, until he issued a challenge for me to investigate for myself before passing judgment on what he considered an innocent pastime. His dare seemed reasonable enough, but had I thought it through I would never have taken it up. After all, one doesn't need to drink poison to know its effect or place one's hand in the fire to know its destructiveness. Foolishly, however, I attended one of the games and rued the occasion, because I learned the reality of the world of demonic darkness. No person should willingly expose himself to such evil. The danger of entrapment is real and severe and can open the door to more serious problems.

The anniversary of Chris's abduction came. I had not seen him for two years and had not spoken to him for a year. In spite of all my adversities, however, I still clung to the prophecy concerning reunion with my son. I even told people about my expectations, but knowing my circumstances they only nodded in pitying forbearance, as if to indulge my groundless fantasies.

Nevertheless, I had no intention of abandoning hope. In many ways I had felt the presence of God more strongly during the months of my anchorless existence than at any time before. I could give no answer then, and probably not now, if anyone questioned me concerning the reason for my trials. I am neither stoical nor fatalistic in passively accepting harsh difficulties, but rather regard myself as exercising positive Christian faith in searching for a biblical explanation. When none is found, I simply apply the tested and proven truth in Rom. 8:28: "And we know that God causes all things to work together for good to those who love God, to those who are called according to His purpose." This I do believe, that God knows the end of things from the beginning of things, and in allowing disciplining situations, always keeps trials in manageable proportions. I do not believe He will permit any difficulty to come upon me beyond my ability to endure.

One of the most difficult features of my severity was that there was absolutely no human instrument to help bear my burden. Physically, I was cut off from Marie, and she had her own problems. The pastors to whom I went for direction and help evidently had never encountered a situation like mine, and either refused or were powerless to assist me. Bob was no help, except for providing me shelter, and for that I was grateful, even though I was constantly fending off his

advances and enduring his possessiveness. There was no
family, for I was totally estranged from every one of them.
So I was alone, feeling the fullest impact of everything the
word must imply.

But my human frailty and loneliness drove me to the only
source of strength and comfort available to me. I do not know
why God delayed His deliverance, but since I was and am
well known to Him, there surely was a divine purpose. I
asked Him why countless times as I poured out my innermost
feelings to Him, and often a mocking voice sought to
persuade me that God took no notice of me, being too busy,
or not caring, or considering me lacking enough points to
merit His attention. I must confess in all honesty that many
times I gave an attentive ear to that bewitching voice, and my
deteriorating circumstances made it easy to do so.

Heb. 13:5–6 became my mainstay, because it contains
God's promise never to abandon me or leave me in the lurch.
As a result, says the writer, I could confidently proclaim that
the Lord is my helper. I had to believe that God was faithful
to keep His promise, even if I didn't feel His presence at some
particularly low times. Would He fail me and risk an
accusation of being untrue?

More months passed, and I still had not secured steady
employment. All my life I had heard the pious-sounding
proverb, "God helps those who help themselves." I never
believed it, because it appears to me that people who can't
help themselves are prime candidates for the help of the
Lord. Anyway, I decided that I would at least try something
by way of cooperating with the Lord. In October I enrolled
in a beauty academy in Buffalo. A student loan and a small
grant got me started. My faithful pickup survived the daily
drive into Buffalo, an hour each way, for a month before it
collapsed. Even in death it blessed me, because I sold its
remains for $450, a stake that was to last the remainder of
the school term.

No choice was open to me except to try to find a place to
stay in the city. Where or by what means I hadn't a clue. Bob

didn't receive the news of my departure very well. In fact, I thought he experienced a paroxysm, and wondered if I should dial 911. He quickly recovered, however, and began a manipulative argument designed to maintain his hold on me. He convinced me that because of my paltry resources I should still rely upon his help and not jeopardize the opportunity to finish school. He assured me that I would be on my own after I graduated and found employment. Making it sound as though he were sacrificing his interests for my own, he announced that he would find an apartment in Buffalo near the school, and I could continue to stay with him. Reluctantly, realizing my dire circumstances, I accepted his logic.

His obsession worsened drastically after we settled in Buffalo, to the extent that he dreaded to let me out of his sight. I was struck speechless one day when he hit me with his decision to enroll in the beauty academy. For a few moments my emotions vacillated between tears and laughter. The tears won.

That's the way it was on Saturday night, November 17. I remember a song saying something about Saturday night being the loneliest night of the week. Maybe it was that feeling of melancholy that prompted me to call my mother, enhanced by the fact that her birthday was coming up on the twenty-third, the day after Thanksgiving. This feeling certainly wasn't guilt over my long silence, nor a sudden rush of filial love, and certainly not the fact that I missed her. If I had waited a bit, the impulse likely would have passed, but I went ahead and placed the call. To my surprise, the number in Maine had been disconnected. Had curiosity not prevailed, I would have abandoned the idea of talking to Mom. Instead I called Margaret, with whom I had not talked in almost two years, and learned that Mom was now living in Cape Cod, Massachusetts.

The apprehension I felt concerning my mother's reaction to my unexpected call was wasted as she was in a friendly, relaxed mood. It didn't take long to catch up on happenings in our respective lives, since neither of us was in any better circumstances than when we last conversed. As a consequence, our conversation was brief, but during the whole of it she kept trying to steer toward the topic of Chris. She had not been interested before, and I had resolved not to discuss the matter of my son with her again. In response to her questions concerning whether or not I had Chris, I informed her that I didn't, and that was all I allowed to be said about him. She was mollified and even seemed genuinely touched when I wished her a happy birthday.

Immediately after my call to her, Mom proceeded to get drunk. As things turned out, it's probably good that at least on this one occasion she was smashed. Otherwise she might never have placed the next call.

# 11

## Fall 1984–Spring 1985
## Buffalo, New York

I discovered how tightly human nerves can be stretched during this brief period of two seasons. A combination of fear, anxiety, suspicion, shame, disappointment, frustration, and intrigue contributed to my overall tension. Roll all those feelings up into a bitter draught and administer them daily for six months, and your system both rejects and accepts the concoction, tossing emotions around like Hulk Hogan discarding opponents in a free-for-all. It doesn't matter which one survives, your nerves lose.

My mother called me within hours after I phoned her. She had no time for preliminary small talk but blurted out the news immediately upon my answering the phone. I think it might have helped prepare me if she had given me some clues or played a guessing game with me, but as it was I didn't have a hint. "I reported your dad to the FBI," was her unceremonial announcement. Her declaration stunned me into silence, and she had to call my name a couple of times to draw me out of my stupor. Instinctively I knew why she had done it, but I had not considered the possibility that she would do it.

"I did it so you could fight for Chris," she told me. I knew what she meant. With the disclosure of my father's secret career, the sword of Damocles was snatched from Mark's hand. He no longer had a weapon with which to threaten me. His whereabouts were unknown to me, of course, but surely a grateful FBI could secure my son for me.

In no way did I plant the idea in my mother's mind to inform on Dad to the FBI. As a matter of fact, because of the history of her indifference, I strove to avoid talking about Chris at all during my previous conversation with her. Mom and I disagree in our respective recollections on this point, but I have no doubt about the accuracy of my account. My

163

personal view is that Mom felt guilty over her part in the
conspiracy that kept Chris from me, or perhaps she was
genuinely moved by my grief. Whatever the motive, it was
done, and I could not restrain the euphoria of excited
expectancy within me. This act of my mother had to be the
pivotal point in my ordeal.

Mom had other information for me. She had told the FBI
about Dad's attempt to recruit me, so they would probably
be contacting me very soon. She added that she had
indirectly warned my father through his brother, Art. I
should have been puzzled by her action in calling Uncle Art,
but strangely enough, I wasn't. It merely confirmed the
suspicion I had entertained for some time that he at least
knew of Dad's secret career and perhaps his involvement
went deeper than awareness.

Every day I expected a call or a visit from the FBI. I was so
highstrung that it took a Herculean effort for me to function
with any semblance of normality. The enormity of what we
were about eluded me, and I took little thought of its
ramifications. My primary concern was the recovery of my
son and putting an end to the nightmarish existence that I had
known for so long.

Days became weeks during which I became a wreck,
managing at best to carry out my responsibilities in a
perfunctory manner. My third Christmas without Chris
passed with no assurance that there wouldn't be a fourth.
I was mystified by the apparent disinterest of the federal
authorities, especially when a spy case was being offered to
them—practically gift wrapped and delivered. Even though
Mom kept encouraging me to have patience, every day I
bemoaned the dullness of the FBI.

I was ready to carry out my own plan by the first week of
January, and I didn't care what the FBI did. I would call my
father with a threat of exposure if he didn't get Chris back
for me. Fortunately, I asked my mother's opinion of the idea,
and among the milder things she said was that it took a stupid
person to think up something that stupid, not to mention that

Dad wouldn't take me seriously. Why not contact the CIA? She classified that suggestion in the "stupid" section as well and told me to calm down.

I did—somewhat—for two weeks. By that time I had no more chewing space on my fingernails and had started on my hair. There was still no indication that the FBI was aware of our existence. Something had to be done before I snapped. By this time Mom herself suspected that something was amiss. She admitted to me that she had gathered courage from a few drinks prior to her call to the FBI. They might not have taken her seriously. She suggested that I might call Walter Price, the same agent in Massachusetts who took her report.

The authoritative tone of his gruff voice over the phone didn't quiet my pounding heart at all. I was already scared. When I finally did speak, my words were dry and brittle as they came out my mouth. At least they sounded cracked to me and in a tone two octaves higher than my normal pitch. I began by identifying myself as the daughter of Barbara Walker, who had reported to him in mid November that her former husband was engaged in espionage activities, and chided him for not taking her seriously. He immediately went on a fishing expedition that caused me to believe that he didn't remember Mom's call at all. Then when he began to put me on the defensive by demanding to know my role in the case, my courage rose along with my dander.

My stubbornness matched his persistence word for word. He kept pressing me for information about my father, and I kept referring him to my mother. Actually I entertained the hope that the information given by Mom would be sufficient and that I would have no further involvement. Finally I told the agent that I wouldn't discuss the matter any more over the phone, but agreed to be interviewed in person. He ended the conversation by politely telling me that he would send a report to Buffalo and someone would contact me soon.

"Soon" turned out to be almost two months. I thought surely I would hear the blare of sirens that very night as top

agents, maybe the director himself, would come rushing in
to hear about a retired naval officer who had been selling
military secrets. In retrospect, I can understand their
skepticism when my mother called. The FBI must receive
hundreds of kooky calls with tips on everything ranging from
the resurrection of Adolf Hitler to counterfeit three-dollar
bills. Add to that a call from an obviously intoxicated woman
charging her former husband with treason, and what do you
have? A vengeful woman getting even with a man who
wronged her by charging him with highhanded crimes sure to
bring serious investigation. The records of such calls go right
into the zero file, something specially designed for wacko
calls, and that's exactly where the report of Mom's call went.

What did Walter Price think of my confirmation of Barbara
Walker's allegations? Are reports concerning spies so common
in Hyannis, Massachusetts, that none of them is investigated?
I could envision the ghost of J. Edgar Hoover fuming at the
inactivity of his boys.

The pressure that I was under as a consequence of the
FBI situation was intensified by the relentless pursuit of Bob,
accompanied by a jealous possessiveness that bordered on
fanaticism. He was constantly hovering over me, even at the
beauty academy, where he had enrolled merely to keep an
eye on me. He listened to every telephone conversation,
including those with my mother and the FBI. Afterwards he
would launch into an enervating diatribe in which he
lectured me about what I should have or should not have said.
I was trapped in an intolerable situation, but I had no choice
other than to endure it until I finished my training. On the
surface, it may appear that I was exploiting Bob's obsession of
me, using him to support me and then dumping him when I
no longer needed him. That assessment of my live-in
arrangement with him is not at all accurate.

From the beginning of our association, I had made it
unequivocally and irreversibly clear that there could never be
any kind of personal relationship between Bob and me, and
I was constantly reaffirming that stance. In no way did I lead

him on or in any other way tantalize him with my feminine
wiles. I preferred to think of our association as strictly
professional, with me earning my way by serving as cook and
housekeeper. Unfortunately he refused to view it that way,
and therein lay the root of the problem.

Once again, I was terribly conscious of my aloneness and
desperately needed someone to fulfill the injunction of
Gal. 6:1 and help bear my burden. All my life I had been
fiercely independent and proud of making my own way. For
almost three years, however, through my own personal
experiences and Bible study, I had learned a beautiful truth
about our need for one another. For various reasons, some
people may try to carry their load alone, but that is not the
biblical way and certainly not the practical way, at least
when the weight of care is as heavy as mine was. Others
claim to need no one but God to help them, pointing to Bible
verses such as Ps. 55:22: "Cast your care upon the Lord, and
He will sustain you." Yet God often works through human
instruments to achieve His ends. A perfect example is in
2 Cor. 7:5–6. When the Apostle Paul was in dire straits,
God comforted him, but not by angelic ministration or other
supernatural means, instead He provided the company of
Titus, a trusted friend of the apostle.

So I looked again to Marie and unloaded on her. She didn't
comprehend what I was trying to explain to her about the
latest intrigue, but at least she was willing to stand with me
and support me. In turn, she shared her troubles with me,
foremost among them being the severe illness of her husband,
which was so drastic that he was sent home from Germany.
She was also grieved by the recent death of her grandmother.
Our mutual trials greatly strengthened our friendship, healing
more rapidly the rift that had occurred between us the
previous year.

It was well into March when the FBI finally contacted me,
telephoning to arrange a time for a personal interview. I had
no idea who or what to expect, but had to conceal my
amusement when I went to the door to receive the two agents

who came. Both of them, Paul Culligan and Chuck Wagner, fit the stereotype of FBI agents right down to the trench coats and sunglasses.

They had no sooner made themselves comfortable and accepted the iced tea that I offered them when the telephone rang. It was Michael, calling to tell me good-bye before he shipped out on the aircraft carrier *Nimitz*. Because I felt uncomfortable in the presence of the agents, I kept the conversation clipped and short, telling Michael to call back later. He left that day and had no opportunity to call again.

Bob came into the room uninvited and remained throughout the interrogation. Although his presence was discomforting to me, I didn't suggest that he should leave, knowing that either way I would be bombarded with his critical opinions once the agents left. If they had objections to his presence, they didn't voice them. I suspect that their impression of the relationship between Bob and me was something other than what it actually was.

If this first session was typical of what was to come, I knew I was destined for many hours of rigorous and thorough interviews. These men were skilled interrogators, trained to manipulate, confuse, lead, discern, and whatever else it took to extract pertinent information. The initial interrogation took the entire afternoon. They questioned me concerning everything I could possibly know about my father's espionage activities. Much of the conversation was directed in such a way as to determine my own possible involvement. Even though they never asked me a direct question about my participation, nor made any accusation, their probe was intensive and rather resentful to me.

Paul and Chuck were not at all belligerent and tried to keep me at ease, but the strain of recalling everything that had occurred, striving to be accurate, was draining me emotionally. It soon became obvious to them that I had no documented evidence to support my allegations, so they concentrated on underlying causes and motives, seeking to determine the depth of my knowledge and why I felt as I did.

The only facts I had, of course, were my own recollections
of conversations with my father and bits of information from
my mother.

Actually I went beyond the bounds of my own knowledge
of the situation and ventured to speculate that my Uncle Art
was involved in espionage prior to my father's activities.
Likely, so I supposed, he was responsible for launching Dad's
spying career. Additionally I implicated Dad's friend, Jerry
Whitworth. (I wasn't certain of his last name; for a while the
authorities looked in vain for "Jerry Wentworth.")

Hours of repetitive questioning left me on edge,
particularly when I became more and more frustrated with
my inability to furnish the solid evidence the FBI desired,
especially where it concerned my uncle and Dad's friend.
Female intuition didn't seem to be a satisfactory explanation
to the doggedly persistent agents, but it was all I could plead.

Within two weeks Paul and Chuck were back with a
scheme to gather incriminating evidence against my father.
I had never expected my involvement to go beyond the one
interview, at which time I told them everything I knew about
the case. From then on it would be the government's
responsibility. Now, however, they were asking me to entrap
my father. I was to call him and lead him into a
self-incriminating conversation by expressing an interest in
returning to the military or possibly accepting a position with
Eastman Kodak. The bait, of course, was the hint of possible
infiltration into classified areas. Naturally, the phone call
would be recorded.

What they were asking me to do was something I had
never anticipated, and my initial reaction was one of
revulsion. I weighed the request carefully for the next two
days, examining all the issues. I felt a natural aversion to the
thought of being used in such a way and didn't know if I
could pull it off even if I agreed to cooperate. I was no
actress, and my father, with whom I had not talked in
nearly three years, was no dumbbell.

Reluctantly I consented to be a block over which my father

would stumble. I was not motivated by a surge of patriotism
and certainly not by a desire to mete revenge on my
father—I still maintained the natural feeling of a daughter's
love for him. On the other hand, I wasn't certain I had a real
choice anyway; I had already committed myself irrevocably in
the matter. As I agreed to the scheme, I experienced no sense
of betrayal but rather harbored a fear of reprisal should my
father discover what I had done. At the same time, however, I
wanted to be successful in putting an end to his illegal
activities.

The agents fit a recorder to my phone, gave me instructions
concerning its use, and left it up to me to make the call
whenever I was ready. I vacillated all day, struggling between
a desire to get it over with as quickly as possible and a
cowardly hesitancy that dreaded to go through with it. My
wavering courage finally steadied long enough for me to
place the call late that night.

My unexpected call after a three-year hiatus completely
surprised Dad, so much so that for a few moments he
uncharacteristically had to grope for words. When
he recovered, it was my turn to be surprised, because he
didn't start bitching at me. Instead, he was friendly and
casual. When he learned where I was (although I suspected
he knew my whereabouts all along), he told me that his
favorite aunt lived in the Buffalo area and that I should
contact her. This innocent reference later provided a valuable
clue to the authorities, although it went unnoticed at the
time.

As naturally as I could, I steered the conversation along the
lines in which I had been coached by the FBI agents. On
the surface at least, my feigned interest in the possibility of
offering my services to Dad's secret career elicited no
positive response, and he refused to nibble at the bait
dangling before him. Lest I arouse his suspicion I did not
pursue the matter.

The intended purpose of the conversation was realized,
however, at least in my estimation, when Dad referred to the

information I had given Mark. According to what he said, my breach of confidence had sent waves of panic far and wide, even up to high places. Relief swept over me as I realized that here was verification of what I had told the agents about Mark's threat. Perhaps now they would accept the entire story as true.

We were less than halfway through a fifty-five-minute conversation when our talk took a nasty turn. Dad reverted to his natural, overbearing self as he began to berate me for having always been an idiot and to assure me that I was destined to remain in idiocy. Once again he alluded to the anxiety that the situation with Mark had caused the network in which he worked. He matter-of-factly admonished me to settle for visitation rights with Chris. In other words, I should do nothing to upset Mark and jeopardize my father's position.

For almost three years I had been denied even a sight of my son, and the nearest my father could get to an encouraging or sympathizing word was a warning to do nothing that might endanger his career as a spy. It's good that I didn't try to cry on his shoulder. I would have ended up with a knot on my head.

True to his egotistic nature, Dad sought to impress me with vivid descriptions of his happy-go-lucky life as a swinging playboy. In his own estimation, he was the world's most eligible bachelor. How could he be bothered by the pain of his daughter? My dad was real slick—the type who would kick a man between the legs and then try to sell him an ice pack.

The agents responded immediately when I informed them that the call to my father had been completed. I sat down to await their arrival brooding over what I had just done and grieved that my father should talk to me as he did. My solitude was short-lived, however, because of an ugly confrontation with Bob, who demanded to hear the tape. When I refused to surrender it, he exploded in a violent rage and thundered heavy threats at me. The man was becoming more difficult, and I was going to have to find a way out of

this intolerable situation. I had less than a month to go before
I finished the course at school.

The contents of the recording of my conversation with Dad
were disgusting to the agents who heard it and humiliating to
me. I had tried to describe my father's character to them, but
evidently they had failed to comprehend his barbarous
heartlessness. As a result, they were taken aback both by
what he said to me and the manner in which he said it.

Dad called me on April 25 and surprised me by wishing
me a belated happy birthday. A part of our conversation dealt
with my mother and a visit that she had just made to Norfolk.
Dad told me that she had made certain threats, but that he
had contingency plans to ensure his protection. These he
promised to discuss with me when I came to Norfolk later.
Actually I knew of my mother's visit and that the FBI was
instrumental in planning it. Its intent was to ease whatever
anxiety might have been caused to Dad by Mom's warning
call to Uncle Art months before.

I had been instructed to activate the recorder every time
my father called, but I deliberately failed to do so on this
occasion. For some reason I just couldn't bring myself to do
it. Informing on my father in the first place seemed to be
an impersonal act, but somehow my involvement was
discomforting to me. When I dutifully notified the authorities
that my father had called but that I did not record the
conversation, they informed me that his telephone was tapped
and that all his conversations were being recorded. Their
deception infuriated me. Why did they have to put me
through something unnecessarily? Or was this their way of
testing me?

I leaned on Marie for support throughout all these
proceedings. Even though she was bewildered by what was
happening and never understood its significance, she never
failed to be a source of strength to me. I'm convinced that
only her prayers and expressions of encouragement enabled
me to survive the pressure building up around me.

That pressure was intensified by the stressful relationship

with Bob. His jealousy and possessiveness quickly reached the point of brain-sick obsession, and I was more scared of him than ever. So far I had been able to handle his outbreaks, but his abuse was becoming increasingly severe, threatening to go beyond the verbal into the physical. I would often spend the night in a vacant storage room in the basement of the apartment building where we lived in order to get away from him when he was particularly upset. Now my hideaway visits were becoming more frequent.

Marie and I discussed alternatives for me to escape from Bob in almost every one of our telephone conversations. We finally settled on a plausible scheme. I would graduate on May 16. The next day, Marie would drive the four hours from Canton, where she was living, and would spirit me away while Bob was out. Packing would be no problem for me since my only possessions were a few articles of clothing and what personal items I had managed to retain.

The FBI requested that I take a lie detector test, and I readily assented. It's a marvel that I was capable of making any kind of judgment at that time. Both mental and emotional fatigue had almost sapped all my reserve of strength. Only my conviction, which I faithfully maintained, that Chris and I would be reunited provided any sense of balance to my otherwise unwieldy existence.

It was a greater marvel that I was able to endure in good order the taxing ordeal of the polygraph test. Not only did I survive, I passed the series of tests to which they subjected me. Evidently they were finally convinced that I was being truthful with them. The man who conducted the grueling session made it less arduous for me. He was a Christian and was especially kind to me. I told him about my long separation from Chris and expressed my belief that I would have my son once all this madness concerning my father was over. He agreed with me! Up to that point the only person, other than Marie, who believed my testimony was a Christian girl who attended the beauty school.

For almost three years I had been doggedly sharing my

faith with scores of people and usually received the same
reaction that Noah did when he predicted rain. The response
of these two people was a much-needed encouragement to me.

There were other interviews with the FBI. During one of
them I met Bob Hunter, who was introduced to me as the
agent from Norfolk assigned to my father's case. I had to
repeat my story for his benefit. In many respects, this was
the worst feature of my dealings with the FBI, repeating the
same details again and again. Surely my testimony was a
matter of record, and I could add nothing of substance. On
their side, they revealed to me no information concerning the
progress of their investigation.

It was now early May, and I was becoming more fidgety as
the date of my graduation approached. Bob sensed something
in the air and attempted to tighten his hold on me by
bullying me. His tactics culminated in his physically beating
me just outside the beauty academy one morning. I didn't
know if I could last another week, even if it was the final one.

Contending with Bob wasn't the most contributory factor
to my turmoil. That in itself would ordinarily have been
enough to crush my spirit, but additionally I had to bear
the enervating strain brought on by recent events. I was
emotionally expended and felt myself to be nearing the
snapping point. Even sleep brought no relief, usually offering
only tormenting dreams that challenged my mental
equilibrium. In the midst of all this agitation, I was caught up
in a battle of another kind, which was much more stern. I
was engaged in a spiritual conflict in which at times I leaned
toward believing that my quest was hopeless, that I was only
deluding myself in constantly testifying to the faithfulness of
God in restoring my son to me. Then the little spark of faith
that had been kindled in me three years before would be
fanned into full flame. I knew that something was going to
happen soon, and I confessed that it would be good.

# 12

May 20, 1985
Canton, New York

I learned that expectancy and shock are not incompatible; it's entirely possible to be positive that something will happen and yet to be stunned when it actually comes to pass.

On Wednesday, May 15, I completed my studies at Peter Piccolo's School of Hair Design. I was now qualified to work in a beauty salon. First, however, I had to escape from Bob. Marie and I had already hatched a plan for me to flee the next day. She called at 3:30 on the morning of the sixteenth to reassure me that she would be there.

As soon as Bob exited the apartment that morning, I hurriedly began to gather my sparse belongings. Marie would not arrive until at least 11:00, but I wanted to spend no more time in the apartment than was absolutely necessary. Besides, Bob could return at any time, and I wanted to be out of his reach.

I made two telephone calls before leaving the apartment. I called Paul Culligan to explain my plans, lest the FBI think I was engaged in something illegal or fleeing my responsibilities. Reluctantly I told him where I could be located. I had not hedged on anything, I had cooperated with the authorities. Now I just wanted to be left alone. They had pumped from me every shred of information I could possibly give them, and I was emotionally wrung out. During the whole time that I was being used by the FBI, I had not received one encouraging word from a single agent in the matter pertaining to the recovery of Chris. They were single-minded in their desire to nab a spy; my own predicament seemed to be of no concern. Although they had the vast investigative resources of the Bureau at their disposal, there was never an offer of assistance in locating my son, much less in retrieving him. Somehow, I regarded myself as being betrayed, although no deal had ever been struck and

177

my cooperation was secured without a price or a promise. I couldn't help but reflect on how my father would consider me brainless for not controlling things to my own advantage, as though betrayal came cheaply.

Probably it was the sense of being used without any thought for my welfare that caused me to snap at Paul when he began to lecture me about an obligation I had to my country to put a stop to my father's activities. Given my emotional state, I was in no mood to listen to that kind of pitch, and I struggled to keep from backsliding into some colorful language that I would have used at one time. I was tired of being manipulated and just wanted to get on with the dominating drive in my life, to get my son. I cut in on Paul's irksome explication with a curt description of my feelings at the moment and then abruptly hung up.

My next call was to Steven in California. I had not called him or written him in a year and a half, and he could not contact me because he had no way of learning my whereabouts. I still felt close to him, however, and was relieved at his delight in hearing from me. I promised to keep in touch, but told him nothing of recent events.

By 9:30 I was ready to leave and in a melodramatic way fancied that in closing the door to the apartment I would put a bitter past behind me. There was even appropriate theme music drifting from an overworked radio in the next apartment—"Lara's Theme" from *Dr. Zhivago* . . . not exactly my name, but close enough. Perhaps it was fitting that I should be theatrical about the business; I had been living a soap opera script for several years.

If there was even a suggestion of reluctance at walking out on Bob without so much as a note of explanation, it didn't surface then or later. I was parading out of "prison" with a defiant lift to my head, finally acting out a moment I had plotted and dreamed for months. Before the curtain dropped, however, the final scene was marred by a pang of hunger that reminded the only character in this drama that she had not eaten and that she still had a long wait. Practicality overruled histrionics and I prudently marched into the kitchen, made a tuna fish sandwich, and filled a paper cup with milk.

Since my grand exit was already spoiled, I took time to check through the apartment once more. I was taking nothing with me that would be a reminder of the unhappiness of the past few months, and I was especially careful to leave behind anything that Bob had given me. He had often presented me with gifts, and I wanted to take nothing that might give him a hold on me. Many days afterward, I learned that Bob persistently called the FBI office, first demanding and then pleading to be informed of my whereabouts. Finally he left messages for me to call him. I never did.

After I had moved my few personal effects to the bottom of the stairwell, nothing remained except to place the key on a table—where Bob would readily see it—and lock the door behind me. I took a last look around and quickly squelched a final thought of leaving a note. Returning to my theatrical flair, I raised my cup of milk with a flourish in a silent toast, took a gulp, and walked out the door.

I went to a vantage point atop a wall across the street. From there I could see Marie when she came and avoid Bob should he return first. Fortunately, Marie, along with her husband Bill, arrived a couple of hours later. We chose to delay a lengthy greeting until later, preferring to get away immediately. My things were loaded in the car within two minutes, and we were gone. Besides the only possessions I had to my name, I carried my bankroll of $70.

As we left the curb, the drama I had been subconsciously playing all morning climaxed with an outburst of tears—only I wasn't acting. My tears were real, and it was many miles before I could stop. I cried because I was free from a difficult situation. I cried because of the emotional pressure that had built up as a result of the ordeal with the FBI. I cried because of three years of empty loneliness apart from my dearest treasure on earth. I cried because I felt like crying, and Marie and Bill wisely refrained from trying to stop the flow.

The long drive to Canton took only minutes, or so it seemed, as I awakened from a tear-induced sleep. I was welcomed into the Hammond home and felt immediate comfort in my cozy room. Even the sound of laboring trains trudging along the tracks just outside my window was music to me. There was promise in the newness of my surroundings, and once again I sensed the familiar stirring of hope within me.

Best of all was the feeling of being again in the midst of loving, supportive friends, a necessity denied me far too long. I knew that Marie had been interceding for me in prayer constantly, even if she lacked opportunity to express more tangible assistance. Now she reaffirmed her belief that Chris would be restored to me, and both she and Bill assured me that we could stay with them as long as I wanted.

Over the next few days I was introduced to Canton, a town of less than ten thousand inhabitants located in upstate New York only a short distance south of Ontario. We toured St. Lawrence University, where Bill worked with the ROTC. It seemed to be a pleasant place to work, and I determined to apply for a position there. In addition, I checked some of the local hair salons and received assurance that I would be able to get a job.

Early on Monday evening, Marie and I were in the kitchen preparing tacos for dinner while Bill was in the next room watching the newscast. With my mind fixed on slicing the onions, I paid no attention to the droning voice of the newscaster. Suddenly my senses were alerted by the urgent tone of the announcer breaking through my inattentiveness. I reacted in time to catch the end of his statement: ". . . Walker, Jr., a former naval warrant officer, was arrested for espionage." I had no awareness of my rushing into the family room; I seemed completely detached from my surroundings. Surely I had not heard correctly. Bill sat impassively watching the television screen, not reacting at all. When my unhearing ears focused on the reality of the situation, Tom Brokaw was still talking about my father's arrest. Finally noticing my stunned look, Bill understood that

the John Walker who was the chief subject of the news was
my father.

Although I had been expecting Dad's arrest, the manner in
which it was accomplished and the means by which I learned
of it were equally shocking to me. I had anticipated an
investigation that would likely take years, during which time
the FBI would painstakingly accumulate a mass of irrefutable
evidence. Then they would simply call Dad in for questioning
as they confronted him with the proof of his guilt. Naively, I
never envisioned a scene with such dramatic suddenness but
supposed that the culmination of the lengthy investigation
would be a quiet apprehension of my father without the
fanfare I was now witnessing.

The reason for my expectations was that I could not believe
my father would be so oxheaded as to be caught in the act of
making a delivery of classified material. In fact, the first
thought that my benumbed mind produced as I viewed the
account of Dad's arrest was a wonder that he could have been
so dull witted, a man who had always been so cocksure about
everything he put his hand to do. He had been alerted by my
mother's warning to Uncle Art. Even though later, at the
instigation of the FBI, she tried to eradicate whatever fear
may have been generated in him by her forewarning, he
should at least have exercised caution enough to cease his
activities for a while. When I later took time to analyze the
situation, I could only surmise that Dad had been engaged in
espionage for so long and found it to be so easy that he
regarded himself as immune to discovery. Further reflection,
however, led me to the conclusion that divine providence
designed the sequence of events; there are no coincidences in
God's plan.

I called Mom immediately following the news of Dad's
arrest. She had nothing to add, having been as uninformed as
I had been throughout the course of the investigation. Each
of us promised to let the other know if we learned any
details. Meanwhile I became addicted to CNN's "Headline
News."

# 13

## May 21–31, 1985
## Canton, New York

During these ten days some puzzles were put together and others were scrambled. Everything was in a state of confusion following Dad's arrest, and the media were scurrying everywhere in a frenzied race to gain information. My part in the case had not been mentioned. Even if it had been, I was tucked away in a place where no one outside the Hammonds knew me. In those first few days when my father's story was front-page news, I had no idea how desperately I needed, and later would crave, the security of that isolation.

On the day after the news of Dad's apprehension broke, Paul Culligan called with a sincere apology that I had not received notification of the events of the previous day prior to their public announcement. He explained that he had wanted to reach me before the evening newscasts but lacked opportunity. To make up for that discourtesy, he and Chuck Wagner planned to visit me the next day to describe what had happened and to seek clarification concerning some cryptic notes that Dad had included in the material left for pickup by his contact.

While awaiting the agents' arrival, I continued devouring the newspapers and viewing the newscasts, but found little to add to the scant knowledge I already had concerning the events of Sunday night and the early hours of Monday. My mother knew no more than I, and I assumed that she would also receive a personal visit from the FBI. When I called Margaret, I found that she was devastated. She had spent a lot of time with Dad over the years, and despite his earlier mistreatment of her, she maintained a close relationship with him. Although I had not asked her to withhold disclosure of my involvement in the episode, Mom had told me she would not reveal that fact to anyone, and Margaret was altogether unaware of the part that the two of us had played. Like many

other of Mom's intentions, however, this one also went
unfulfilled. Margaret, now knowledgeable of my role, was
extremely angry the next time I called her. Our exchange of
words became more and more heated until she finally hung
up. All of us were in a state of confusion and turmoil, and
this was not time to attempt an explanation to Margaret.

Paul and Chuck arrived late on Wednesday morning, having
left Buffalo quite early to start the long drive. From their
report to me, supplementing what I had learned from the
media, I was able to piece together the sequence of events
relative to Dad's arrest.

My father's telephone, as I had known, was tapped. In
scores of calls over a period of several weeks, listening agents
heard a great deal of obscenity in various forms, but nothing
incriminating. Suspicion was aroused, however, by two calls
that Dad received on Friday, May 17. The first was from a
relative informing him of the death of his favorite aunt near
Buffalo and of her funeral on Sunday. Dad expressed his
sorrow over the death, but told the caller he would be unable
to attend the funeral because of a pressing business
commitment in Charlotte on Sunday. A few minutes later,
another relative called to berate him for not postponing his
business trip and to urge him to change his plans. Expressing
his regrets, Dad adamantly declared the urgency of his trip
and explained that he was the only one who could attend to
the business.

Later that day, when he learned of the calls, Bob Hunter,
the agent in charge of Operation Windflyer, the code name
given to the case, thought it strange that my father would
refuse to attend the funeral of someone for whom he
professed such fondness. His suspicion was reinforced by
Dad's reference to this same aunt in the transcript of my call
to him, made the previous month at the request of the FBI.
He had encouraged me to visit her, but now he couldn't be
bothered to go to her funeral. Hunter sensed that Dad's
business trip was actually a drop of secret documents and
ordered a thorough surveillance to be carried out on Sunday.

He was right and the surveillance was thorough, both from the air and on the ground. Instead of heading for North Carolina, Dad drove furtively to a rural area in Maryland, not far from Washington. There he was observed depositing a bag which later proved to hold 129 secret documents, any one of which was devastating to American military security.

The government agents muffed the opportunity to nab Dad's contact when one of them removed a strategically placed 7-Up can, my father's signal that the delivery had been made and that the area was clean. The contact, who was spotted as he drove along the route, was Aleksei Gavrilovich Tkachenko, a KGB officer operating under the guise of third secretary of the Soviet embassy. When he failed to see the prearranged signal, he kept on driving.

Had it not been for its tragic seriousness, the scenario would have reached almost comic proportions when my father returned to the area later that night in a frantic but fruitless search for his payoff. FBI agents lurking only yards away clearly saw him and heard his confused and angry curses as he thrashed through the brush looking for a package that had never been left. What must he have been thinking in his baffled state? The bag he had deposited was gone, so evidently the pickup had been made. Had he been double-crossed by the Soviets? He returned to the drop site several times before giving up.

It was after midnight when my frustrated father reached his room at the Ramada Inn in Rockville, Maryland. At 3:30 A.M. on Monday, an FBI agent, posing as a hotel clerk, telephoned Dad's room, apologetically reporting to him that someone had crashed into his new van. Could he come to the lobby to handle some matters pertaining to insurance? Waiting in a room down the corridor toward the elevators were Bob Hunter and another agent, both with drawn weapons. Danger signals were buzzing in Dad's senses. Leaving his room, he first checked the corridor and the stairwell and then quickly returned to the room. Within moments he was out again, heading for the elevators.

Suddenly he was confronted by the two agents pointing their guns straight at his heart. It would have been in keeping with Dad's love affair with the flamboyant for him to reenact the gunfight at the O.K. Corral, and, true to his character, he had his own gun leveled at the G-men. For a few seconds, it was an uneven stand-off, until Dad prudently decided he had a better chance of talking his way out than shooting his way out. Dropping his gun, he smirked and began to wisecrack. The agents weren't at all receptive to his banter as they roughly shoved him against the wall and handcuffed him. The final indignity was administered when one of them ripped his prized toupee from his head and flung it to the floor.

The substance of this report, aside from intricate details, I had already heard or read. None of the news accounts, however, described the contents of the bag that my father had left at the drop site. In addition to the secret documents, there was a letter written to his KGB contact. In the letter he referred to four different people involved with him in espionage activities, using the code letters "S," "D," "F," and "K." Culligan read the references to see if I could identify any of the people. Knowing what I did, and listening to the excerpts, I suspected that "D" was Jerry Whitworth and "K" was my Uncle Art. Concerning "F" I hadn't a clue. ("F" turned out to be Dad's half-brother who was never associated with him in his illegal affairs.) But sickening comprehension grew within me about the identity of "S," and I tried to stifle it by repeatedly denying the possibility that it was my brother. That the FBI considered "S" to be Michael was obvious, since most of the confiscated documents had been stolen from the *Nimitz*, on which he was stationed, and the letter stated that "S" had provided them. (I didn't know that agents in Norfolk had already discovered a notebook in Dad's house positively confirming the identities of everyone involved.) With a sagging heart, I slumped in my chair, still denying Michael's involvement, but not believing my own words. The agents told me that Dad had asked for a payment

of a million dollars, a paltry sum for the exchange of his own
son, his brother, and his best friend.

Immediately following the agents' departure, I called my
mother and learned of her conviction that Michael was "S."
Our fears were confirmed within hours when the newscasts
announced Michael's arrest aboard the *Nimitz*. The image
of my manacled younger brother being led down the steps of
a plane at Andrews Air Force Base on Saturday, May 25, is
forever etched on my memory, and I will always ache for
him. I was overcome by his humiliating treatment, knowing
that he was not a criminal but the victim of his father's clever
manipulation. I had not seen my brother in five years, and as
I viewed the pathetic scene on the television screen, I wanted
to reach out and embrace him and somehow help him to
understand that I never intended to hurt him. All I could do
at the time was to weep bitterly. I thought back to his
telephone call to me on the occasion of the first visit I
received from the FBI in Buffalo. The timing of the call was
good or bad, depending on one's point of view. Had he called
only minutes earlier, I doubtless would have shared with him
the fact that Mom and I were in contact with the FBI
concerning Dad, not because I thought Michael was involved,
but simply because as my brother I felt he should know. As
it turned out, no other opportunity presented itself.

I more than anyone understood how Michael had been
influenced by our father, and I loathed my Dad for carefully
grooming him for spying. He arranged for my brother to
live with him in Norfolk when Michael was only sixteen.
He spared no expense in stimulating in him the greedy
tendencies that we all have by nature, lavishing upon him
everything that a teenage boy could want. There were
surfboards, stereos, a snazzy pickup, an extravagant
allowance, and an abundant supply of sex, alcohol, and
marijuana. Michael's character was far from exemplary
anyway, and now he was directed into a profligate lifestyle
that was totally self-centered. He surely thought that he must

have been translated straight into his distorted version of
heaven. By the time he was eighteen years old, he was as
deeply entrenched in epicurean decadence as his father. Not
only did John Walker ingratiate himself to his son by spending
lavishly upon him, but he began to work on his mind as well.
Dad chipped away at whatever convictions Michael had by
making off-handed remarks about the corruption rampant in
the government and tantalizing him with hints of how he had
beat the system and made easy money.

As I contemplated Michael's fearful situation, I felt
wretchedly hopeless. I could do no more than fall to my
knees and pray, barely able to talk through my heaving sobs.
Boldly I pled for God's mercy and deliverance. As a result, I
felt led to write Michael letters of hope and encouragement,
testifying to him of God's grace. At first, he never responded,
but I knew he was reading them and I persisted in writing.

The FBI assigned another agent to me out of Syracuse,
which was much closer to Canton than Buffalo. I had
supposed that my part in the case was over with the arrests
of Dad and Michael and the later arrests of Uncle Art and
Jerry Whitworth, but I discovered that there were to be many
more interviews and court appearances. I never sought the
publicity that was soon to come, nor desired it. All I wanted
was to secure my son and remain in the safe obscurity of
anonymity.

The new agent was aloof and totally insensitive to the fact
that the man who had just tripped the country's alarm
system was my father. Like so many others who knew only
the FBI's role in cracking the spy ring, he failed to see the
whole picture from the proper perspective. I do not mean to
minimize the investigative efforts of the FBI, but had they
not been tipped off about my father, he might still be
practicing the secret trade in which he engaged for at least
seventeen years. Despite his coarse vulgarities, he was in
many ways a brilliant man as well as a very cautious one. In
short, he was an excellent spy, as evidenced by the testimony
of Vitaly Sergeyevich Yurchenko, the KGB defector. The

KGB considered the Walker ring to be the most valuable in its history. The cryptographic material delivered by my father enabled the Soviets to decipher every secret American message they intercepted. Who knows what further damage he could have caused had he continued operating. As it was, it took divine providence to overrule human blunders.

The reticence of the FBI in responding to my mother's first call, and later to my own, is difficult to fathom. Despite the meticulous thoroughness of the surveillance of my father on May 19, he still managed to elude the observers for several hours, even though he was unaware that he was being watched. The removal of the 7-Up can was inexcusable. Even though all the credit has been given to the painstaking efforts of the FBI in connecting Jerry Whitworth with John Walker, the truth of the matter is that the identity of Whitworth would have remained unknown had I not informed the FBI of his existence. The previous year, Whitworth, evidently wanting out of the spy ring and willing to trade exposure of my father for immunity from prosecution, had written a series of letters to the San Francisco office of the FBI, signing them with the name "RUS." His identity remained an enigma until my mother's and my interviews with the FBI.

While many people attribute happenings to luck or chance, I see the hand of God at work. There are no coincidences within the framework of the sovereignty of God. He did not wind the universe up like a toy and then leave it to run, or run down, by itself. God is very active in directing the affairs of people and nations. In fulfilling His designs, God uses many human instruments, most of whom have no realization that they are serving His purpose.

At the end of May, both my mother and I were scheduled to appear before a grand jury hearing in Baltimore. Four years had passed since I last saw her, and I was eager to visit her again, especially to learn what she might know about the situation that I didn't know. Michael's wife Rachel, whom I had never met, would also be there.

Paul Culligan drove me from Canton to Baltimore in his car, and during the trip we had ample opportunity to talk. This man had been extremely kind to me during the many hours of interrogation I had undergone. He had displayed an understanding sensitivity to my moods, and rarely lost patience or grew angry with me. Through it all he had made a valiant effort to maintain his novel sense of humor—often he succeeded. Even on the way to carry out the disagreeable mission in Baltimore, I responded with medicinal laughter. In turn, I shared with him how I had grown in my relationship with God, and had remained steadfast in my belief that Chris and I would be reunited. He listened to and affirmed what I told him.

The years had not been kind to my mother, or rather she herself abused the passing of time. I was unprepared for the physical change in her. I tried without success to conceal my shock at seeing how the years of unrestrained alcoholism had taken their toll. She was only in her forties, but had the haggard look of a much older person. She had once been a beautiful woman, but liquor had taken her beauty and gave only distress and disgrace in return. She had been crying when I saw her, and had been since she learned of Michael's arrest. I mixed my tears with hers because we both knew that only a miracle would spare him from life imprisonment.

I had been in a state of numbness ever since I learned of Dad's arrest. Now a gnawing queasiness threatened to overwhelm me as the next morning Mom and I walked the short block from our hotel to the courthouse. If anything, she was more unsteady than I. Reporters and cameramen were teeming before the entrance to the building. Fortunately, we were unknown to them, so we proceeded unbothered to the office of Assistant U.S. Attorney Mike Shatzow. He met with each of us separately, prompting us concerning the type of questions we could expect to be asked.

Finally, after what seemed to be an indeterminate wait, it was my turn to testify. I tottered on Jell-O legs to the witness stand and faced the stern jury, hoping to detect some visible sign of sympathy. I found none. My uneasiness vanished, however, as I simply recounted my knowledge of Dad's activities and his attempts to recruit me as an accomplice.

While my mother was testifying, I was directed to an office where I would be issued a plane ticket back to New York. I was also told that Mark had been subpoenaed and that I would be able to see him if I so desired. Of course I did! My whirling mind computed dozens of questions to ask him that somehow might aid me in my quest to get Chris. Meanwhile, as I waited for the private meeting to be arranged, I noted several people whom I recognized as associates of my father. Most of them wore bewildered countenances that spoke of disbelief of what was transpiring. None of them gave any indication of recognizing me.

Three grievous years had crept by since I had last seen my husband, and if I expected him to be changed in the least, I was mistaken. He was as irresponsible as ever, telling me that he had no money for cigarettes and no way to get back home, which I learned was still in Baltimore. Here was a man who had deprived me of my son, causing me to walk through the darkest abyss of the lowest hell, and he was asking me for money! I had every right to tear into him with a screaming vengeance, but the rage never surfaced. Instead, I quietly handed over the money he needed. I don't know why I acted as I did. Foolishness, perhaps, but maybe the best way to combat his hardened insensitivity was by matching it with a calm spirit that betrayed nothing of the cowering distress within me. Actually, I had never wasted time plotting sanguinary revenge against this man, and wished him no harm. All I wanted was to realize a mother's right to be with her child.

Striving not to appear too obtrusive, I asked Mark about Chris. In fact, I felt ready to burst with the fullness of nearing my objective to reach my son. Carefully, however,

I worded my questions so as not to arouse Mark's suspicions about what I hoped to accomplish. He was happy to oblige, and gave me his father's address, saying that he and Chris were staying there.

He lied, and my son's whereabouts were still unknown to me. In spite of his deception, I felt myself to be near the end of my ordeal. In the words of the J. B. Phillips translation of 2 Cor. 4:9, I was "knocked down, but not knocked out."

# 14

## May 31–June 14, 1985
## Baltimore, Maryland

These fifteen days were filled with confusion and pain, but they were also a time that brought a prophecy near its fulfillment. In my case, several worn-out axioms proved themselves true.

- Things did indeed get worse before they got better.
- Things were darkest before the dawn.
- Low ebb had to be reached before the tide turned.

Satanic forces must have sensed my strengthened belief that my determined journey was approaching its conclusion. Everything around me scoffed at my faith, loudly proclaiming its absurdity and deriding me for blindly clinging to my thin strand of hope.

There certainly was no outward evidence to the contrary. I still had only faith and no substance in my mission to recover Chris. Michael's arrest and certain long-term imprisonment weighed heavily on me. And in spite of all the anguish my father had caused me, I still grieved for him, knowing what he must be going through. Uncle Art and his wife were also present at the grand jury hearing and were on public display. All in all, it was a dreadful scene for everybody.

Mom and I were refused permission to visit with Michael, a decision that neither of us understood and which greatly upset us. We did manage to spend a little time with Rachel though. Our first meeting was less than cordial; she evidently blamed me for tearing down her dream castles. Her acidlike stare burned holes through me while her coldness plugged them with ice. She doubtless had failed to consider the fact that her happiness had been destroyed not by a decision I had made but by one her husband had made.

Nevertheless her frosty attitude thawed enough to join us for dinner after Mom detailed for her exactly how I became involved in the case. Following dinner we visited with Rachel in her hotel room. She showed us pictures of Michael and talked of their life together. It was a sad time for the three of us.

The press was starving for information and seemed to be interviewing anybody they recognized as having a connection to the participants in the spy ring. Fortunately for my mother and me they had not yet learned our identities and were more interested in Rachel. As a consequence, we were spared a media nightmare in Baltimore, a blessing to us because neither of us was in a condition to deal with persistent newshounds.

The hotel room that Mom and I shared was a refuge after the tiring events of the day, and we talked well into the night. A part of our conversation that especially upset me concerned my mother's admission of an affair with Dad's brother, Art. Instead of consisting merely of a clandestine tryst or two, the *affaire d'amour* was long running, spanning a period of ten years. My anger was kindled not so much by my mother's indiscretion but by her hypocrisy. For years before I left home, I listened to her claims of purity while she was lambasting her husband for his unfaithfulness. While I still viewed her as a victim of my father's shameful abuse, I now saw her as violating her own marriage by playing house with her brother-in-law. The sins of both of my parents were detestable, and they greatly contributed to the devastation of the lives of their children.

Mom left for home the next morning, but I was not scheduled to leave until the afternoon. Alone in the hotel room, I looked out the window at the surrounding buildings. For a long time I stood staring at the courthouse, contemplating the fate of my father and my brother. It was impossible for me to think of them as the average American citizen would, as traitors who betrayed their country out of greed, spies who deserved to die. In no way could I ponder

the case with that kind of detached and impersonal
objectivity, nor did I wish to. "Spy," "traitor," "betrayer,"
"subversive"—these offensive words seemed curiously
inappropriate to the men of my family, especially to my
younger brother. The very sound of these words was
uncompromisingly harsh, and yet there was no denying their
applicability to those concerned. As that reality embedded
itself in my understanding, I began to weep, slowly at first,
but then with soul-shaking wails.

My grief for others soon evolved into lamentation over my
own hardships, which in turn were transformed into anger
toward God for not getting me out of the mess in which I was
floundering. I could understand getting caught in the
quagmire because it was as much my doing as anybody's. But
what bothered me was the fact that I had been faithful in
giving everybody, even strangers, a positive testimony of how
God was going to restore my son to me, and it had not come
to pass. Why did God let such an opportunity to display His
greatness slip by? At the same time why was He allowing
me to appear so foolish, believing when there was no hope?
And, as a P.S., why God had given me such a rotten father
who had brought unspeakable misery to his family and to
others? Where was love? Love cannot be defined in words; it
can only be known by experience. Thus far I had been
deceived with cheap imitations. The only real love I had
known was what I had given to and received from my son,
and that privilege had been lost for so long I could scarcely
remember it. I wasn't even certain that I had really known
God's love. Maybe I had been deceived there also. What had
I gained in professing faith in His faithfulness?

I uncorked my soul and let all its emotional contents pour
out. Might as well be honest with God, I figured, because if
He is who and what He says He is, He knew my thoughts and
feelings anyway. Maybe it was the weakness of the moment,
given the strength-draining context of the past few days, that
prompted my outburst of disloyalty. Or perhaps all the time
I had been relying solely on the efficacy of my own words to

bring about the reality of my confession of faith rather than on the power of the energizing Holy Spirit within me. Whatever occasioned this display of faithlessness, it served to unveil some serious defects both in my understanding of and commitment to the will of God. Even then, as I spent my anger, I made a common mistake that must grieve the heart of God every time one of His children is guilty of making it. The mistake was that of failing to wait around for an answer. After I told God off, I busied myself getting ready to leave for the airport, failing to allow Him opportunity to minister comfort and understanding to me. Clear answers were readily available to me in the ever-present hotel Bible provided by the faithful Gideons, but I took no thought of it.

It's good that God is longsuffering with us, enduring our imbecilic, faith-shattering tantrums. I must have appeared to Him as the classic yo-yo Christian with all my ups and downs. On the other hand, perhaps He saw me as I was—a spiritually immature, confused, and frightened child who knew only to tell God how she felt and to wonder out loud why it was taking Him so long to kiss my hurts and make them all right.

Lessons already learned were soon recalled and fresh insight was added in order to give me a clearer glimpse of God's way of dealing with us. For one thing, I found that faith is not a bridge over troubled waters but a pathway through them. God's people are not promised deliverance from trials, but they are assured of deliverance through them.

Another lesson I learned is that "not yet" doesn't mean the same as "no." Surely one of the most difficult things for us to bear is the silence of God when we ask Him *why*. We feel that we can go through just about anything if only we know why. I believe that God doesn't often answer the question of why—at least that was true in my case. It isn't that God has no answer. Instead, we probably could not comprehend it if He did give us an answer. Besides we must learn to trust Him without knowing why. Questioning God is calling Him into account, asking Him to explain Himself. Beyond our spiritual nearsightedness, God has a reason, and we can trust His heart when we can't see what His hand is doing.

I do not mean to say that I have fully discovered God's reason in dealing with me as He did. I believe I have in part, but it is enough to know that He always works toward a purpose, and that purpose is always beneficial to me and to others.

Picking up my shattered pieces after my sparring match with God, I made my way to the airport and on to Syracuse. While waiting for my connecting flight to Canton, I punished myself with an overcooked and overpriced hot dog at the snack bar. While I was pretending that I was feasting on prime rib, my assigned FBI agent and one of his cohorts approached me, out of breath and out of sorts. They had been looking everywhere for me and were most anxious for my welfare. Why didn't I answer the page? I didn't hear it. Had anything unusual happened? (Well, I had fought a furious spiritual battle in my hotel room that morning, but I don't think that's what they meant.) So I said no. Notice anybody suspicious? Only the robed fellow with a shaved head who tried to pin a flower on me.

It was time to get serious. Did they really think I was in danger? Could be. From publicity-seeking maniacs? Russian hit men? My revenge-minded father? Actually, I was too tired to worry about it. Anyway the two G-men kindly stayed with me until I boarded my plane. They never did tell me the cause of their alarm.

Marie met me at the airport in Canton. Although she was excitedly panting for information, she graciously went unfed until I had a full night's sleep.

The next morning I shared everything with her, at least the factual events. There was no way I could convey to her the impact that the happenings had on my emotional state. I tried to express my feelings, but my inadequate stammering only made what had happened seem strangely remote and impersonal. As usual, however, Marie listened with understanding and open-hearted support.

The press quickly found out about me. My whereabouts,
which had been unknown by anybody other than the
authorities, somehow became common knowledge. As a
result, a steady stream of unfiltered news reporters flowed to
the Hammonds' house seeking interviews. I wasn't looking
for publicity, so I customarily asked Marie to express my
regrets and send them away. Instead, she basked in the
limelight and fed them choice tidbits of information. When I
voiced my objections and asked her to desist, she responded
that she had said nothing of significance. By then, however, I
had learned that members of the news media would often
take small pieces of factual knowledge and turn them into
full-blown accounts, usually inflated with fabrications. I
figured that the less said would mean less fuel for the fire.

I failed to reckon the persistence of journalists grabbing at
anything connected with the Walker case on which they
could build a story, especially a hot item like my own
involvement. The pressure mounted around me, and I knew
I was dangerously near to a cave-in. I needed help
desperately, particularly since I was brooding more and more
over the fact that even though my father and my brother
were both imprisoned, I was no closer to recovering my son.
The apparent injustice done to me kept gnawing at my
insides. The 700 Club telephone prayer line had been a
mainstay for me in the past, but now I wanted the advice of a
strong, mature, knowledgeable, and wise counselor to lead
me out of an unbearable situation. Marie suggested that I
might need some legal advice as well, and she just happened
to be aware of a person who met all the qualifications I
demanded. I called Pat Robertson, in addition to his spiritual
acumen, he also holds a law degree.

The closest I got to talking with Pat was to be connected
with Joyce Radford, his secretary, who refused to put me
through to him. By this time I had been given the shuffle
by a whole series of office workers who didn't know what to
do with me except to push me along to the next level of
authority. I was intemperately agitated. Why should a reputed

man of God be so elevated that it was beneath his lofty position to talk to a commoner pleading for a word of instruction? It never occurred to me that there were thousands just like me. If Pat talked individually to every one of us, he would have time for nothing else, even on a twenty-four-hour shift.

So when Joyce offered to pray with me, I sort of flipped my lid. Not that I didn't appreciate her offer or value her prayer, but in my undiplomatic manner, I let her know that a one-minute prayer wasn't going to straighten out a corkscrew condition like mine. In my desperate state, I interpreted the proposal to pray to be a way of putting me off, a nice way to pacify a pest. In an effort to convey to her the gravity of my need, I spilled out the story of recent events in my family, including my separation from Chris. She was not untouched by my tearful narration, but she wasn't moved enough to let me talk to her employer. Mentally I numbered her among the disciples who thought they were doing Jesus a favor by keeping needy people from Him. The best she could do was to promise to get a message to Pat, so I left my name and telephone number.

Still dissatisfied, I called CBN again. This time, I was transferred to the institution's chaplain, David Jones, an elderly man who is surely one of the kindest and most gentle people on earth. He prayed for me and then spoke the most encouraging and uplifting words I had heard since my testing time began. He reminded me that trials are occasions for rejoicing and showed me how I could be a light in the abysmal darkness engulfing my family. Then in a prophetic word, he declared that members of my family would be saved and that it would be "the greatest love story ever told, page after page." When I told Marie about what had been said, she interpreted the last part to mean that I would write a book. Sure, Marie. Meanwhile I could try to earn a living by selling sandbags to Saharan nomads.

Actually I decided to be a little more realistic about seeking a livelihood, so I stayed close to home and applied for a job in the placement office at St. Lawrence University. Sort of ironic, I guess, that I hadn't been able to find a job for myself, and now I was trying to convince people that I was qualified to find jobs for others. Strangely enough, I felt certain of employment there.

Meantime I was kept busy trying to dodge the press corps, and not being too successful at it. There was always a congregation of reporters at the house, and I had to run the gauntlet from the car to the house with a barrage of questions fired at me every step of the way. Some of the more aggressive snoopers banged on the windows and shouted for me to come out.

One Thursday, a couple of weeks after my return from Baltimore, Marie and I escaped the newshounds for a much-needed diversion of window shopping and taking the dog for a grooming. My dear friend knew my moods well and had a knack of matching the need of the moment with a curative ministration. It was good to be able to forget the problems for a little while and laugh our way into silliness. That's the way it was on this particular afternoon, but we sobered quickly when we again had to face the bevy of reporters awaiting our arrival at home. "I've got to get away from all this," I squawked to Marie as we successfully shut ourselves in from the crowd outside.

My expressed desire was not long in being realized. Messages were flashing on the answering machine, one of which was from CBN. Instead of Pat Robertson, the call was from Jackie Mitchum who identified herself as the guest coordinator of the "700 Club." I didn't know what a guest coordinator was, but I returned her call immediately.

Jackie asked me if I would be willing to come to CBN and talk to Danuta Soderman or Ben Kinchlow, who were cohosts of the "700 Club." I understood her to be presenting me with an opportunity to receive prayer and counsel from one of them instead of Pat Robertson, so I readily agreed, provided that Marie and her two boys could accompany me. I really needed Marie's support, and of necessity the boys would have to come since there was no one to take care of them during our absence. (Bill was away on duty.)

This condition was acceptable to Jackie, but she had a request of her own. Could we leave that night on an eight o'clock flight out of Syracuse if she had prepaid tickets waiting for us? By then it was three in the afternoon and I made some hasty calculations. Syracuse was two and a half hours away, and we would need at least an hour to get ready for the trip. We would be able to make it with a little cushion of time. Marie expressed hesitation about the rush, wanting to wait until the next day. As for me, I felt a compulsion to leave that day and was ready to go alone if necessary. When Marie saw my determination, she agreed to the arrangement.

One problem remained, however. Even though our airline tickets would be provided, we had no money to fuel the car for the trip to Syracuse and for whatever incidental needs might arise. Not to worry. Not when there is a generous paper boy in the family with $30 saved from his route. This from Marie's son, Jonathan, to be reimbursed, of course.

Ten minutes later I was ready, waiting for the others, when a call came from Molly Young, an assistant to Jackie Mitchum. I was mystified when she said that she needed to ask me some questions. She explained that fact sheets were compiled on each guest who appeared on the "700 Club." The information would provide leads for the host doing the interview.

Contrary to some of the later reports, I did not ask to be on the "700 Club," nor did I desire the publicity. Not until Molly called did I know that the true purpose of my trip to Virginia Beach was to be interviewed on television. What I wanted and had expected were spiritual counsel and practical advice, not hype. Nevertheless, I felt impelled to go. Perhaps I could at least find a few days of solitude away from the reporters.

I was a wrung-out dishrag by the time we were winging our way to Virginia. Not only had the constant tension of the past three weeks been emotionally exhausting, but I was

having physical problems as well. For two weeks I had been
hemorrhaging intermittently, a disorder that so far had
confounded the doctors and which caused me no small
anxiety. In addition, tension was building in me over my
decision to appear on television as I wondered about the
timing. How would my family react?

Midnight was drawing near when we were finally settled
in our room at the Omni Hotel in Norfolk. I had to be ready
for a 7:45 pickup the next morning.

Friday, June 14, was a gorgeous day. In a little while the
beaches would be thronged with beet-red tourists not
sparing themselves in the hope of achieving a golden
one-day tan. I sat sedately in the Green Room contemplating
the forthcoming interview. I was not nervous, and my only
concern was that the questions be pointed and direct since
we were allotted a mere seven minutes for my complicated
story. The interview, I was told, would not be shown live that
day but would be taped.

Seven minutes quickly became twenty. Danuta Soderman
did the interviewing, and things seemed to go well. I was
surprised that I could relate so much of my story in such a
brief time, even managing to feature prominently the
two-year-old prophecy that had been spoken by the CBN
counselor concerning Chris.

Following the taped conversation with Danuta, Marie and I
were led to the office of Guy Evans, a jocular but efficient
lawyer in CBN's legal division. There the three of us watched
a replay of the interview so he could became familiar with
the basic outline of my case. He expressed his confidence
that I would soon have Chris but was puzzled that I didn't
know where Mark lived. When I explained the circumstances
and mentioned that I had briefly seen Mark at the recent
grand jury hearing in Baltimore, Guy told me that since Mark
had been subpoenaed, the office of the assistant U.S. attorney
would have his address. Could a simple telephone call secure
for me something for which I had been seeking for two years?

It could and did. I placed a call to Mike Shatzow's office and within minutes knew Mark's address and telephone number.

During lunch, Marie and I resurrected the strategy that had been put to rest two years before. I was ready to pursue it that very day. The officials at CBN had provided me with a rental car so I could show Marie and the boys around the area. I determined that I would widen the area a little bit, say, as far as Baltimore.

Before we left on our venture, we met once more with Guy Evans at his request. What he told me then radically changed the direction of my plans following the recovery of Chris. He shared with us that he had been in earnest prayer for me when the Lord impressed upon him that I indeed would get Chris back, but I should leave on the mission as quickly as possible. He assured me that it would be in order to take the car. To my astonishment, he generously offered to provide a refuge for Chris and me with him and his wife in their large country home. There we would be sheltered from the media and be provided for until I found a job and could afford to rent an apartment. I could even have the use of one of his cars.

Until that moment I had every intention of returning to Canton with Chris, where I expected to be accepted for the job at St. Lawrence University. Now the offer of assistance from Guy Evans caused me to consider the possibility of remaining in Virginia Beach. Marie and I briefly discussed this alternative, and both of us felt that it sounded like the Lord's provision. Whether or not I received help from Guy, I would not be returning to New York.

Late that afternoon a stout-hearted search committee set a resolute face toward Baltimore. It was comprised of an overwrought young mother, her giddy coconspirator, and two willing but bewildered boys, aged eleven and eight. Our only weapon was a firm conviction that what we were about was right, and no posse ever ventured forth with a greater dedication to the successful completion of its mission. Nor was one ever less prepared or experienced.

# 15

Saturday, June 15, 1985
Baltimore, Maryland

This was a day of anguished fulfillment. We were the first breakfast diners at the International House of Pancakes. I should have been worn to a frazzle after the events of the previous day and the few restless hours of a night in a cheap motel catching snatches of fretful sleep. Nevertheless I was animated by the false energy of adrenaline that had me higher than the most potent pep pills. The collapse, I knew, was bound to come, but meanwhile I hoped there was enough vigor left in my reservoir of strength to galvanize my will power for a few more hours.

That same force had supercharged me during the long drive from Virginia Beach. For most of the trip, Marie and I were strangely silent, each lost in her own thoughts. As for me, I was positively certain that I was only miles and hours away from the end of a bad trip that had been going on for almost three years. Both my son and I had been heartlessly denied the joy of any kind of relationship, even the privilege of seeing each other, during his most formative years. Now, however, I would take him back the same way he was taken from me.

Even though I had steadfastly confessed restoration of Chris all through our separation, more negative thoughts than ever were now trying to crowd their way into my mind. I entertained quite a few of them before realizing their faith-destroying mission and kicking them out. Realistically, however, many negative questions demanded answers that I didn't have. What if Mark had given a fake address to the authorities? What if he and Chris were not at home, or had moved? What if Chris were not alone long enough or not in a suitable spot for me to take him? Worst of all, what if Chris remembered nothing about me and fought me or withdrew from me? Anything could go wrong, and we could be on a fruitless errand.

211

At the same time I was not going to allow any zero thinking to nullify my faith. I had prayed and believed too long; shed too many tears; endured too many heartbreaks; walked through too many fires of Gehenna; and dreamed too many dreams to have my belief start crumbling now. Of this I was convinced: I could not experience that hellish nightmare again, certainly not in my own strength. Only by the grace of God had I lived out the last three years, and if anything rendered reunion with Chris impossible, then I doubt that I would have the effrontery to presume upon that grace any longer. Nor would I desire to; it wouldn't be worth the effort merely to exist. At least, that's what I thought, and I didn't want to find out.

Several adverse incidents abetted the negativism in attempting to dissuade us from fulfilling our mission. We were physically tired even before we began the trip, and weary people don't make the best traveling companions. When two washed-out and tense carmates blame each other for getting lost in the Washington, D.C., area, they can get a little bit testy with one another—which is what we did, until Marie turned the first cheek, shaming me into apologizing for rudely snapping at her.

More was to come. Neither of us had the foggiest notion what part of Baltimore we were supposed to be in, and the hour was late when we arrived. After being pointed in the right direction by a policeman, we began looking for a motel in the general vicinity of Mark's residence. The first three were booked solid. The $75 rate at a fourth place, a run-down establishment, encouraged us to keep driving. At the next place we were greeted by a parking lot party of swaggering drunks and bold prostitutes, so we moved on. It was 10 P.M. before we secured a room, and the boys immediately plopped into bed exhausted. Marie and I weren't too tired to check out the local eatery.

There was no phone in the room, so we couldn't receive a wake-up call, and we had no alarm. Wanting to get an early start in order to find Mark's apartment, I set my mental alarm clock for 6 A.M. I was wide awake at that time. I was also awake at 5, 4, 3, and 2 A.M., fitfully dozing in between.

I was highly agitated and did not feel the lack of sleep. I paced the floor nervously while the others were getting dressed, repeatedly asking Marie if she really thought we could pull it off. To calm me down, she led us in prayer for the successful completion of our plan.

Breakfast was satisfying, but I soon regretted the three cups of coffee that I drank. I didn't exactly have to pass through the waters that Isaiah talked about, but they had to pass through me, and in most unfavorable circumstances.

The area where we were was slightly familiar to me; I recognized it as being near the place where Mark's father used to live. Still, it took some scouting around and finally asking directions at a service station before we found Old Stagecoach Road. After that, we soon were parked next to Mark's apartment building. It was 7:30 on a quiet Saturday morning.

The silence in the car was profound as we gazed at the object of our long search. I could scarcely believe that my son was somewhere within the walls of that building. Sensing my rising anxiety, Marie placed a gentle hand on my shoulder, either in reassurance or to restrain me from impetuously dashing into the building.

I couldn't hold back my tears any longer. The memory of Chris as an adorable, curly headed, two-year-old Mama's boy played on my mind. I saw him vividly as I remembered him that last morning when I left him with the babysitter. I imagined that I could feel the pressure of his chubby little arms around my neck, and I actually felt my cheek for the evidence of his impatient wet kiss. I could still smell his crisp morning freshness before it was soiled by a hard day of playing. I heard his tinny, high-pitched voice chirping out his goodbye to me, and while it once had been music to me, the three-year echo of it had been a funeral dirge. I had kept alive these and a thousand other sounds and sights because they were all I had of my little boy. He was now five years old, and I had no idea how much he had grown or how long or what color his hair was or if he had suffered any injuries other than the ordinary bumps and bruises that an active child experiences. I had missed spending three birthdays and three

Christmases with him. I wondered if he asked about me, and
if so what explanation was given to him.

The sound of Marie's voice pulled me back from my
reflection. It was time to get practical. The battle plans had
already been made, but we had to reconnoiter the field.
Eleven-year-old Jonathan was our designated spy, mainly
because Mark had not seen him in five years and likely would
not recognize him should he see him. Jonathan bravely
marched into the building to map out the situation. Mark's
apartment was on the third floor facing the yard. We had a
clear view of the apartment and the playground from our
vantage point in the parking lot, but we could not be seen
from Mark's window.

Our plan, first devised two years prior, was totally lacking
in imagination. We planned to wait until Chris came out to
play, get him into the car, and speed away. It was simple and
workable—if Chris came out to play. It also meant no rain,
and dark low clouds were beginning to sweep over the
vicinity. We began to pray, audaciously reminding the Lord
how He had rebuked a storm that threatened to swamp His
boat. All we were asking was that He delay a measly little
rain cloud. Whether it was the efficacy of our prayer or the
course of nature, the skies cleared and the sun came out. We
refrained from a vociferous demonstration of thanksgiving
for fear of attracting too much attention.

I was prepared to wait all day if we had to, but
unfortunately my bladder, tested by my overindulgence of
coffee, wasn't as patient as I. By 8:30 it sternly insisted that it
could stretch no further and demanded proper attention. My
crossed legs subdued its urgings only temporarily, so I tried
other diversions—humming "Onward Christian Soldiers,"
engaging in upper body isometrics, twisting my body into
grotesque positions, and other exercises. Marie, seeing my
discomfort, thought I had another case of bad nerves, and
once more put her hand on my shoulder. Billy came to the
rescue with a simple, "Mom, I gotta go!" I quickly
volunteered to take him. The only problem was that Marie
also confessed to hearing nature's call.

We were in a predicament. The nearest facilities that we knew of were at the gas station where we had asked directions. If all of us went at the same time, we might miss Chris if he and Mark came out. How could I forgive myself if I lost the opportunity to recover my son because I had to take a pee break? Jonathan proved equal to the challenge again. He stayed behind to keep the apartment under observation while his three weaker coconspirators left on an unavoidable errand.

We were gone only as long as necessity dictated and quickly returned to the stakeout. As we approached the apartment, my attention was riveted to a small boy cavorting on the lawn in the presence of an adult couple. I thought it might be Chris, but before we were close enough to tell, Marie startled me with a sharp command to duck out of sight. Mark was standing on the balcony of his apartment watching the scene below. I was petrified and remained stonily upright in the car seat. Any sudden movement on my part might catch his attention, giving him an unfair warning. So I sat motionless, trusting that Mark wasn't wearing his glasses.

Fearing that Mark might see us, Marie parked the car out of sight at the end of the building instead of returning to our original site. She too thought that she had caught a fleeting glimpse of Chris as we passed by, but from our new vantage point we could not see. After a few moments I insisted that we return to the original parking spot where we had an unimpeded view of the entire scene. There I saw my son for the first time since he had been abducted. I could hardly believe he had grown so much, and the thought of how much of his development I had missed momentarily suppressed the joy of the renewed sight of him. My first impulse was to jump out of the car and run to him, but Marie's restraining hand on my arm checked me. Chris was not alone; he was in the company of the older couple, who I learned later were his babysitter and her husband. Only minutes passed before they left and Mark called Chris back into the apartment.

It was more than I could handle. Whatever bogus composure had held me together shattered; I came unglued. I bewailed the fact that we had left earlier because in so doing we probably missed our only opportunity to take Chris. Marie's gentle and firm logic, however, finally began to break through to me. She reasoned that there was little we could have done given the presence of the couple with Chris. Besides, God would not have brought us this far to disappoint us. She was right of course, and strengthening faith slowly seeped into my inner being as I recalled the Scriptures and the prophecy that had been my Gibraltar for so long. Still my recollection was tainted by the memory of the oft-repeated dream of coming near to Chris but never reaching him.

A torturous hour crawled by, and the sun burned away the morning coolness. Nothing had disturbed the stillness surrounding the apartment building except the comings and goings of a few tenants. Soon, however, a few children trickled into the playground, and we prayed fervently that the sounds of their activity would draw Chris outside to join them. Suddenly, I found myself saying aloud exactly what we had been praying for: "Chris will see these kids playing and will come out."

More minutes passed, and I contradicted my confession of faith as I began to discuss with Marie alternative plans, finally narrowing them to two. Either Jonathan himself would go up and invite Chris to come out and play, or he could ask one of the other boys to try to get Chris outside. We settled for the latter course on the slim chance that Mark might recognize Jonathan.

We watched apprehensively as Jon approached the children, acting as though he belonged in the neighborhood. We could see him talking to one of the boys, pointing toward Mark's apartment. Just as the boy was shaking his head "no," Chris came bounding out of the building. All our manipulative efforts had been for naught, and we could have spared ourselves that anxiety if only we had resigned ourselves to God's way of carrying out His purposes and not tried to run ahead of His timetable.

Marie acted quickly, as though we had rehearsed the scene dozens of times. Starting the car, she drove as unobtrusively as possible to the exit of the parking lot, parallel to the playground. By this time Jonathan was leading Chris toward us, and they were only steps away from my side of the car when we stopped. The look of uncertainty on my son's face betrayed the second thoughts he was having about straying from the playground with a strange boy, especially when an unfamiliar car stopped within feet of them.

There was no time for persuasion or explanations. I had to reach Chris in a instant, before he bolted in fear, fulfilling my recurring nightmare of failing to get to him when he was so near. I opened the car door and leaped out, spanning the short distance to Chris in the blink of an eye. Lifting him in my arms, I could only hoarsely whisper through my tears, "Chris, I'm your mother." Whether it was the simple trust of a child, a dim memory sparked to life, or whatever, his response was to put his arms around my neck, put his cheek to mine, and squeeze tightly. I had only a split moment to savor the delight of that embrace, but it became to me in that tick of time a treasure that will last a lifetime. Instantly, the clasp of those little arms locked around me freed me from the lonely pain that had tortured me for three years.

Barely ten seconds had passed before I was in the front seat of the car with Chris; Jonathan joined his brother in the back seat. Marie had the car in motion even before the doors were closed. As we rounded the curve in the street and sped out of sight, Mark was racing down the stairs, three steps at a time.

We had successfully enacted a plan devised two years before, but I was unprepared for Chris's response. He was bewildered, but not terrified. Mainly he was concerned that his father would be angry at him for leaving, and was disappointed at missing a picnic and going to an amusement park. He started to cry as he asked me to take him back. I thought I had done the right thing in taking him away but began to wonder if it was fair to Chris to subject him to another upheaval. Perhaps I was being selfish and was catering to my own needs without considering the effect on him.

His cries and entreaties broke my heart, and I told Marie to turn around and go back. I loved my son too much to allow him to go through the confusion he was experiencing. Marie flatly refused to change directions, pointing out that to do so would actually be a betrayal of my love for Chris, a denial of God's purpose, and a contradiction of Chris's best interests.

As usual, she was right and her sound reasoning prevailed. The Lord was soon to confirm that we acted correctly. Meanwhile Chris seemed to be accepting me as his mother.

Four hours later we were back in Virginia Beach. As soon as we settled in our hotel, I called Jackie Mitchum in Los Angeles, on location with the "700 Club," which was to be telecast from there all the next week. She arranged for all of us to fly to California the next day where Chris and I would appear together on the show. I was thrilled to have the opportunity to share nationwide the fulfillment of a prophecy.

The rest of the afternoon we spent at a mall buying clothes and toys for Chris, using the remainder of the expense money CBN had given me. He was understandably baffled by all that had happened. To both put him at ease and to give Mark an explanation, I called Mark. He indeed had seen us speeding away, and although he was obviously angry, he maintained a civil tone. There was nothing he could do since I had committed no crime in taking Chris, as he well knew from his own action of three years before. He did help to make the adjustment for Chris as smooth as possible, assuring him that they would see each other soon.

I placed one more telephone call that night. Los Angeles was only an hour's trip by plane from Steven. He had been a long-distance friend to me during the pandemonium surrounding the arrest of my father, and I wanted to see him, especially to share with him how God had done His work in my life. He assured me that he would come to Los Angeles while I was there.

It was still early in California when our travel-weary group arrived on Sunday. The frenzied pace of the past few days had taken its toll on me, and my physical strength was further enfeebled by my persistent hemorrhaging problem. At the airport Jackie told us that she and her sister, Margie, would be taking us to Disneyland that afternoon. All signs of fatigue immediately vanished—except from me. My preference was to stay in bed the rest of the day, but in no way would I deny Chris the opportunity to make up for the outing that I had caused him to miss the previous day. So my enthusiasm was more than pretense as I covered my discomfort and agreed to the trip.

Something weird happened as we were leaving the terminal. A man who looked like he was freaked out on drugs walked straight toward me, stepping on my feet, apparently without realization. Jackie intercepted him and asked where he was going. "I'm on a mission," he mumbled. "What kind of mission?" she questioned. Seeking me out with unfocusing eyes, he responded, "A mission for Satan," and ambled away.

I did not dismiss the encounter lightly. Whether or not that man himself posed a threat to me, I interpreted it as a warning, recalling the words of 1 Pet. 5:8: "Be careful—watch out for attacks from Satan, your great enemy. He prowls around like a hungry, roaring lion, looking for some victim to tear apart." God had done a wonderful and powerful work in my life, and I knew that the enemy desired to silence the testimony I planned to give.

The trip to Disneyland failed to accomplish all that I hoped it would. While the other boys reveled in the excursion, Chris remained somewhat withdrawn. I suppose I couldn't expect a two-day reunion to bridge the gap of three years' separation, but I was grieved at his confusion and prayed for wisdom in dealing with it. A positive sign encouraged me that night when a tired little boy confessed to me that he had a good time and then hugged me and whispered, "I love you, Mommy." I wept a long time that night, but my tears were comforting as I lay looking at my beautiful son.

Jackie had two separate reports that were considerably disturbing to me. The first concerned a compromising videotape of my sister-in-law, Rachel. An employee of CBN purported to have a copy of the tape in which Rachel supposedly performed a provocative striptease. The man wanted me to give him money in exchange for the tape. I had no money—and why would I want the tape anyway, unless the man thought I would want to spare Michael embarrassment? And why was a professed Christian engaging in blackmail? I didn't know then that the tape issue would be raised again, and that I would be accused of something terrible.

The second report was that Pat Roberston, having seen the taped interview of the previous week, was skeptical about my identity. Since the interview had gone so smoothly and since I was very composed and confident, he felt that I had to be an actress posing as the daughter of John Walker. I don't know how he expected the daughter of an accused spy to act or what she should look like, but to allay his suspicions, I cooperated with the head of CBN's security unit as he investigated my identity. Pat evidently was satisfied because the next scheduled interview was conducted as planned.

While I was having make-up applied in preparation for the program, one of the producers made an encouraging confession to me. After the first interview she said that she pitied me for clinging to a two-year-old prophecy that would not come to pass. Now that I had Chris, she said that she had learned that one could not dictate the time frame in which God must do His work. She also said that her faith was greatly strengthened. I soon heard similar accounts from many people who viewed the programs.

Steven arrived that afternoon, and the two of us took Chris to the beach. While Chris was busy playing in the sand, Steven and I began a conversation that lasted through our return to the hotel and well into the night. We had once declared our love for each other, and the attachment was still strong. We both knew, however, that there was no future for us together.

Steven finally returned to the room he was sharing with the boys, while Marie and I stayed together. There was no rest for me because my hemorrhaging had gotten much worse, and I was both uncomfortable and frightened. Sometime during the night I called Steven, and he took me to the emergency room at the nearest hospital. The cursory examination I received was inconclusive, and I was given a few pain pills and dismissed.

CBN had provided us with an eventful trip to California. For the time being my troubles seemed to be far away. I knew though that trying times were bound to come. I was right.

# 16

Summer 1985–Summer 1988
Virginia Beach, Virginia

These three years were a bitter-sweet time of emptiness and fullness, but through it all I felt the presence of one who promised never to leave me, and as a result experienced an ever-increasing faith. "And they lived happily ever after" is a phrase that might be appropriate for fairy tale characters, but it doesn't apply to many real-life people and certainly doesn't fit my own situation. Some of my severest tests have been endured during this time, beginning with the recovery of Chris.

But new difficulties have meant new opportunities, and big battles have meant glorious victories. The old cliché warns there is a thorn with every rose, but I prefer to see a rose with every thorn. I am no masochist, and my ability to endure pain and heartache is low, but my Father knows my resistance capability and never permits any adversity to slip beyond that point. It's interesting that the endurance mark moves ahead a few degrees with every trial successfully met, not in my own strength, of course, but in the energizing strength of "Christ who gives me the strength and power" (Phil. 4:13).

I do not mean to suggest that the Christian life is a ceaseless struggle of ups and downs in which permanent victory is never to be realized. I simply mean that, at least in my own life, a certain refinement had (and still has) to be accomplished, and that discipline is often a chosen instrument to bring about the alteration. I believe that God loves us as we are, with all of our imperfections, and He accepts us as we are when we come to Him through Jesus Christ, trusting not in our own merits, but casting ourselves resourceless on His mercy and grace. But God loves us too much to leave us as we are, so by His Holy Spirit, who indwells us, he begins to shape us into the image of Christ. Chipping away the accumulated crud of years of selfish, wayward living may be a slow and

painful task, but it is a necessary one. Then comes the
sandpaper and the buffing cloth, polishing us into a full
reflection of the image of Christ. So we follow the admonition
to "be happy, For when the way is rough, your patience has a
chance to grow. So let it grow, and don't try to squirm out of
your problems. For when your patience is finally in full
bloom, then you will be ready for anything, strong in
character, full and complete" (James 1:2–4).

The California interlude would have been idyllic had it not
been for my baffling physical condition. The people at CBN
lodged us in a beautiful hotel, fed us with sumptuous food,
introduced us to celebrities, provided us with entertainment,
and saw to our general needs. Yet my chronic hemorrhaging
was getting worse, and I felt myself weakening. Much-needed
sleep, induced by a sleeping pill that Jackie gave me on the
flight back to Virginia, helped tremendously.

Upon our arrival in Virginia Beach, I called Guy Evans, as
he had instructed. Plans had changed in the few days I had
been away. Instead of staying at his house, Chris and I would
have the use of an apartment owned by CBN, but only for
thirty days. This was far short of the previous offer of room
and board and the use of a car until I was financially stable.
Guy and Jackie were able to extend my "lease" to sixty days,
but how was a single mother going to find a job, get an
apartment, buy a car, furniture, clothing, and other items all
in two months? I wondered if I had made the right decision
in remaining in Virginia when I had a certain amount of
security in New York. A firm job offer had been made by
St. Lawrence University, and Chris and I would have a home
with a family that truly loved us.

Although I wavered, I stayed. The hardest part of the
decision was saying goodbye to Marie and her two boys at the
Norfolk airport. No Jonathan had been a truer friend to a
David than she had been to me. I'm convinced that I would
not have survived beyond Louisiana had it not been for the
faithful and prayerful support of this woman, who never once
expected or asked anything in return from me. Most certainly

I would not be where I now am were it not for her presence in my life. Clouds of disagreements and conflicting personality traits often obscured the sunshine of our relationship, and sometimes we hurled verbal daggers at each other, but she was a living example of "a friend who sticks closer than a brother" (Prov. 18:24). No Hollywood production, with its artificial tears, could rival our farewell scene at the airport.

I felt obligated to tell Rachel about the tape and the attempted blackmail, so I called her. Although I did not offer one word to suggest that I was judging her, she immediately took a defensive stance. I assured her that I had not seen the tape and had no intention of viewing it. My only concern was to warn her that the tape was in the possession of someone who evidently was going to try to exploit it, and that she perhaps should consult her lawyer. After I explained how I knew of the tape's existence and gave her the name of the man who was trying to peddle it, she abruptly hung up without even thanking me. What she did with the information I gave her proved to be a consternation to me.

Immediately after settling into my borrowed apartment, I applied for a job at CBN and soon was granted an interview for a faculty secretarial position in the School of Biblical Studies. The people at CBN had expressed a concern that I be shielded from the media and others who might seek me out, but the job was not guaranteed to me. I went through the normal channels in applying and then waited for the results of the interview. After several snail-like days of antsy waiting, I was offered the position, beginning on July 22.

On my first day at work I was informed that my borrowed car had to be returned. Guy Evans told me that he would give me a car that he had received as a bonus from CBN. He changed his mind, however, and Operation Blessing presented me with what appeared to be a reject from the salvage yard, a Honda Civic that had more than 100,000 miles on it. I couldn't complain, though, because at least I had transportation. The next year I gifted another ambulatory person with the same car.

I had no difficulty finding an apartment when my sixty days in the CBN apartment passed, but I didn't have a single article of furniture. So I was taken to the warehouse of Operation Blessing to look over furniture that had been donated. Most of it looked like it had been deliberately left behind when the Goodwill truck made its collections. Embarrassed, Guy suggested that I rent essential furniture at his expense for two months. After that, I didn't know how I could manage to furnish the apartment on my woefully meager salary. In addition to a total lack of household items, I owned only the clothes I brought from New York—a pair of jeans, a few tops, one outfit suitable for office work, and a few undergarments. Chris had only the few articles of clothing I bought before going to California. With the remainder of the small honorarium that CBN had given me, I purchased additional clothes and toys for him.

Again, with the privation I was facing, I questioned the wisdom of remaining in Virginia instead of returning to New York. Marie did not share my indecision; she straightforwardly ordered me to get back. The prospect was tempting, but I still felt compelled to stay. Inexplicably, I sensed that God's purpose was still unfolding and that He was going to work things out.

There were varied reactions to me among my new acquaintances. On the one hand, I was astounded at the generosity of some people who provided me with household items and other necessities. I received enough money and gifts of furniture to furnish my apartment comfortably. These people and others of kindred frame immersed me in their loving concern and prayerful support. With few exceptions, most notably the benevolence extended to me by the Hammond family, I was unaccustomed to this kind of treatment, especially from those who weren't approaching me with their own schemes of banking on my notoriety.

On the other hand, I was equally surprised by the resentment of some malcontents and grumps who were so choleric in their own dispositions that they begrudged any degree of well-being in others. Some of these disgruntled dyspeptics were piqued merely because people were generous to me, while others protested that CBN was giving me preference when they knew of cases more deserving than mine. Instead of rejoicing with me that my needs were being met, they tried to steal whatever quietude had come to me. I still wonder if such people know that 1 Corinthians 13 and similar passages are in the Bible.

Other problems beset me as well. My physical affliction steadily grew worse. I consulted a succession of doctors, but none was able to diagnose my difficulty. There was a particularly ugly scene in the office of one doctor who wanted to perform an operation on me that, according to him, would stop the bleeding but not necessarily correct its cause. Sometimes I am prone to fall from the grace of a sweet disposition and backslide into the nasty temperament that my street education fostered in me. I tend to suffer this relapse when I am under stress and people or circumstances irk me. (This is only one of many areas in my life where the Holy Spirit is still applying the sandpaper.) This was one of those times. As delicately as I could, so as not to appear too coarse, I told the doctor what he could do with his butcher knife and then stormed out of his office. The last thing I heard was his angry shout that he was the doctor and knew what he was doing. Fine, but do it to somebody else.

Finally, to my vast relief, I was directed to a doctor who gave me a thorough examination and traced my malady to an ovarian cyst that had been aggravated and enlarged. Its remedy required only a simple treatment of hormone pills.

Greater than financial and physical problems was the tension that both Chris and I experienced in adjusting to our new life together. I had to learn to be a mother again, not to a totally dependent two-year-old, but to an independent-minded five-year-old who suddenly was transferred from the security of the only environment he could remember into the unfamiliar surroundings of a strange city with a woman he could only dimly recall as being his mother. The three-year gap in our relationship, especially at the tender age of my child, required the construction of a sturdy, well-founded bridge to span it, and it would demand time and attention if it were to endure for a lifetime. I could not afford to make many mistakes, and I was a novice in building that kind of bridge. I would have to spend much time searching the instruction book and consulting its author.

First, I had to take steps to gain legal custody of Chris and seek protection against a recurrence of Mark's action three years before. Therefore, I filed for child custody in Virginia Beach, while at the same time Mark sued for divorce and child custody in Maryland. Things went in my favor from the very beginning of the legal process. The courts decreed that the case should be heard in Virginia Beach since Chris was residing there. At the first hearing I was granted temporary custody until the case was decided. As I was leaving the courtroom, I overheard Mark complaining to his lawyer why they even bothered to make an appearance. It was evident that Mark had been convinced that he would be given custody of Chris.

Later, while I was completing some required paper work, Mark approached me, his eyes glazed with the telltale signs of a marijuana high that I recalled so well. I had once given myself unreservedly to this man, but his irresponsible selfishness had crushed into nothingness the love that I had for him. That total disregard for anyone but himself had caused me to go through three years of an anguish that defies adequate description. Now in the midst of a custody battle he was destined to lose, that same selfish pattern emerged. He had denied me not only the right to see my son and the privilege of talking to him on the phone but even the comfort of knowing where he was. Now he was asking me to give him the prerogatives of a father that he had refused to allow me as a mother. By no means would I withhold Chris from his father, so I gave Mark permission to see him at specified times but stopped short of agreeing to joint custody, as he proposed.

Before the case reached its conclusion in the courts, Mark yielded custody of Chris to me with the proviso of certain visitation rights. A local newspaper quoted him as saying, "I'm tired of her hiding behind God." I was gratified that he could recognize my dependence on God. What better place to hide when one needs shelter?

In spite of all the adverse factors that threatened to flatten my inflated joy of having Chris with me in the beginning of a new life, I could be thankful for a multitude of blessings. In record time God was attending to my needs, and I was beginning to focus on my blessings rather than my curses.

Contrary to insinuations in various publications, I never sought to capitalize on the Walker spy case, although many opportunities were immediately offered to me. I received a lucrative offer from the editors of one of the sleazy supermarket tabloids which specializes in sensational exposés, true or not. For $10,000, all I had to do was appear in one of their television commercials, repeating the statement, "Read about how I turned in my spy father to save my son." I flatly rejected their overture.

In addition, I received contacts from publishers interested in my writing a book for them. I would be untruthful if I denied being thrilled to have the opportunity to tell my story and quickened by the possibility of realizing monetary gain from it. As a result, I seriously entertained these offers, and finally signed a contract with a well-established company for a guarantee of $150,000. In my own defense, I must say that I was concerned with relating a positive story that would bring glory to God by underscoring His work in my life. Unfortunately, the publishers were not interested in the spiritual side of things. Consequently, the person engaged to help me write the book took an entirely different approach than the one I wanted, completely ignoring my emphasis on spiritual matters. After a long delay, the publishers broke the contract, declaring that my way was "too religious." I still could have the $150,000 by agreeing to write the story the way they wanted it, filled with all kinds of smut.

There were also opportunities on television, and I appeared on most of the major talk shows and news programs. Never did I invite myself to be a guest on anyone's program; I don't even know how to go about it. Nor were these appearances financially rewarding, since I usually received little more than traveling expenses. My motivation was to have the opportunity to present my side of the story in an effort to correct fabrications that were being spoken and printed as truth.

It didn't take me long to discover that most people see and hear only what they want to, regardless of the facts. I also discovered how powerful and biased the media can be when they present facts from their own perspective and interpretation, slanting the truth in the process. If what I said was a contradiction to their reports, then the intimation was that I was in error. Still, I took advantage of as many opportunities as I could in order to tell the story from my point of view, which in most areas connected with the Walker case was usually a firsthand account.

The grand jury hearings no longer involved me, but I was subpoenaed to testify at the trial of Jerry Whitworth. My father had agreed to testify for the prosecution as part of a plea-bargain. The agreement was that Michael would receive a twenty-five-year sentence instead of life imprisonment.

The trial was held in San Francisco. I had not yet faced any of the defendants during the hearings, but now I would be testifying against Jerry as he was there looking at me. On the flight west I considered the irony of the matter, and wondered how I would feel as I testified before him. He had been my father's friend for many years, but it wasn't until Dad's visit to me early in 1982 that I got to know him very well. We had gotten together a couple of times that year following Dad's visit. I accepted a dinner invitation from him, thinking that perhaps I could gain some insight into my father by talking to his friend. Jerry's wife was not present during that meeting.

Nor was she present when we next met, this time at his

house. I should have known that his interest went beyond
having an innocent tête-à-tête with the daughter of an
old friend, but since he had been a gentleman during our
previous engagement, I had no reason to suspect that he
would be otherwise this time. I was mistaken. He had some
proposals to make concerning the evening's entertainment
and came on to me like a sex-deprived Lothario.

I countered his suggestions with some of my own, but he
wasn't too interested in praying. I did succeed, however, in
sharing with him my Christian convictions, stirring his
interest enough that he engaged in theological arguments
with me well into the night. At the time, he appeared not to
have been affected in the least by my witness—but now I
wondered. He had sent anonymous letters to the FBI in 1982,
not long after we talked. Maybe something was stirring
within him; he indicated in the letters a desire to quit the spy
business.

There was no occasion at the trial to see him privately,
even though I strongly preferred to testify to him instead of
against him. I didn't feel that I was betraying him and had
no close ties to him, but I was grieved to know that he would
spend the rest of his life in prison.

One highlight of this period was Steven's commitment to
the lordship of Jesus Christ. When he saw me in Los Angeles
and became aware of how God had wrought visible changes
in my life, he was influenced to become a Christian. He has
rapidly matured in his faith since then. Seeing his growth
has brought much joy to me and the knowledge that I was
instrumental in his conversion experience has been immensely
satisfying.

Near the end of 1985, I finally received a letter from
Michael. He had indeed received my letters and had even
read them. In his brief note he told me that he really wanted
to talk to me and would call me on a certain day. I was
ecstatic. For months I had prayed for an opportunity to talk
personally to Michael and try to help him understand what
had happened. So on the appointed day I waited with flushed

excitement, which gradually waned as the day grew old and
no call came. Nor did Michael call the next day or the day
after. By then, I had resigned myself to the fact that he
would not call.

At length, another letter arrived, this one hotly irate in its
tone. He scathingly castigated me for harassing his wife about
the videotape she had made. The tape, he wrote, was
intended only for his viewing pleasure while he was at sea,
and there was nothing lewd about it. He went on to
enumerate other justifications of the tape, none of which was
necessary, because I had made no judgment of it in the first
place. The primary reason for his anger, he stated, as well as
the reason for his failure to call, was that I had tried to sell
the tape. (I later learned from Michael that Rachel had
twisted my conversation with her to make it appear that I was
trying to profit from the tape.) He concluded his letter by
telling me there would be no further communication between
us and that I should not bother coming to visit him—my
name was excluded from his visiting list.

My initial reaction was bristling anger at his unjust and
false accusation. I truly regretted having mentioned the tape
to Rachel. It was none of my affair to begin with, but I
thought she should be warned about the threat of blackmail.
She either misinterpreted my call or blatantly misrepresented
me to Michael. Why she would do the latter, I had no idea.

The flare of blazing anger was short-lived to be replaced by
helpless sorrow at the prospect of losing all contact with my
brother. I was inclined to sit down immediately and write a
letter to clarify the part I had played in the rotten mess, but
prudence dictated that I pray about it and let God handle it.

This was the best way by far, because the healing of my
relationship with Michael began shortly thereafter with
another letter from him. He asked me to come for a visit! I
was at the prison in Petersburg, Virginia, on the earliest day
I could visit. I had envisioned being able to see Michael only
through a glass partition, conversing by means of
microphones, with no physical contact at all. To my pleasant

surprise, there was no barrier of any kind between us, and we were able to sit together and converse freely.

I embraced my brother with genuine affection, and he responded—hesitantly and awkwardly—but he responded. We had not seen each other in more than five years and wasted no precious time on this first visit in idle pratter. There were scores of questions and answers from both of us, so we plunged right in. I learned from him the details of his arrest and the feelings that he was harboring. He heard from me the story from my own perspective, as without self-justification I chronicled the whole sequence of events. Michael expressed guarded satisfaction with my account, but still withheld his full forgiveness of Mom and me. This restraint painfully revealed to me the fact that he held me responsible for his dilemma rather than himself and our father, who certainly bore primary culpability. Our conversation did include a brief discussion of spiritual matters, in which I encouraged Michael to give serious consideration to his relationship with God.

Strangely enough, the subject of the videotape barely received mention. On a subsequent visit, however, we discussed the matter candidly and at length. By that time, Rachel had begun to show signs of separating herself from Michael, and he was able to be more objective in his observations. He acknowledged to me that he had been deceived and questioned many things his wife had told him. She had even reported to him that I often called her at home asking to speak to "Roxanne." I had no idea who Roxanne was until Michael explained that it was Rachel's stage name when she danced at a strip joint. Supposedly she was dancing in order to earn money to visit him in Italy when the *Nimitz* berthed there. According to her, I was using the name to vex her. Michael had not known that she was performing in a club and soon discovered the true circumstances in which the videotape was made. I assured him that I was unaware of any of his wife's activities, including the use of a stage name, and that I had nothing to do with the dumb tape. I was chagrined later when the accusation carried over into print with the publication of a book that claimed to relate the true facts of the Walker family.

Before 1986 became history, all the principals in the Walker spy ring had been sentenced. Most likely, Michael is the only one who will ever walk outside prison walls as a free man. With good behavior, he will be released before he reaches the age of forty, regardless of whether or not he is paroled.

Shortly before Christmas of that year, Michael became a Christian. I had been faithful in interceding for him in prayer and witnessing to him in letters and personal visits, and fruit was finally produced. His faith is daily subjected to all kinds of tests in the harsh bleakness of his existence, but I am confident of God's keeping power. Michael at first was incarcerated at Petersburg, a drive of only an hour and a half from Virginia Beach, so I was able to visit him regularly. Early in 1988 he was suddenly transferred to a prison in Lewisburg, Pennsylvania, and I have been unable to see him as before. We correspond regularly, however, and our love for each other continues to grow.

I have neither seen nor spoken to my father since his arrest, because he has made it repeatedly clear that he wants nothing to do with me. Sometimes I grow pensive and think of the wonderful father he once was, when it was easy and natural to laugh, and I pronounce curses on whatever demons bartered for his soul. All I can do is pray for him. Do I feel guilty? No.

My mother and I have maintained a wobbly relationship, mostly because in her continuing alcoholism she has allowed the truth to become distorted. Regrettably, she entrusted herself to an agent who is only a cut above a con man. In attempting to enhance the value of Mom's marketability, he has unscrupulously sought to discredit me, flagrantly branding me as a liar.

The relationship between Margaret and me was frigid for many months following the disclosure of my part in the developing Walker case, but a gradual thaw has restored our

closeness. We still have our awkward moments, but we can
discuss everything openly and be honest with each other. She
lives in Norfolk, and we enjoy seeing each other often. It's
easy once again for us to laugh together.

Cynthia is still in Massachusetts with her son and our
mother. We never really had an opportunity to develop the
enduring nearness and dearness that siblings should nourish,
but I fervently hope that will change.

Christopher has been spared much of the upheaval that one
would normally expect to attend the circumstances that
whirled around him, and he is a happy child. I strive to make
up for the years we missed and try to show him love in
everything I do, including discipline. I want him to
experience things denied to my childhood and to be secure in
the shelter of both my love and God's love. He is peculiarly
sensitive to spiritual matters and prays beautiful prayers.
Every day we have our special time together with the Lord.

Chris still feels a tug between me and his father. He spends
most major holidays and a large portion of the summers with
Mark. That division has created a dilemma for him, and the
day may come when he will decide of his own volition
whether to continue with me or go to his father. I can only
pray that by the time that stage is reached, he will be so
firmly grounded in Christ that I need not fear his choice.

I have not seen Marie since our tearful separation at the
Norfolk airport in June 1985, but we "reach out and touch"
by telephone on a regular basis. The bonds of our friendship
have not loosened a fraction, but have actually tightened
their hold on us. We are together, and it will always be that
way. When I need her, I know she will come. How can I
adequately express thanksgiving to God for the blessing of
such a friend?

In the midst of the turmoil surrounding the legal
proceedings of 1986, I seemed to be climbing out of the
deep valley where I had been wandering for so long with
only occasional glimpses of the sun above the shadows. I had
my son; I had my job; I had friends; I had a lucrative book

contract; I had a divorce from an unfaithful husband with whom I had not lived in five years; and I had the promise of marriage to a man who seemed to fulfill everything I could want in a husband. But I was deceived again. One who has survived the tribulations that I walked through should be impervious to heartbreak, but my invulnerability didn't extend to my heart. I gave myself to this man in full expectation that we would share a lifetime, and we planned a ministry together. Foolishly I entrusted to him all the money I had left after prepaying for our wedding and a honeymoon package to Hawaii. I even paid for my own engagement ring. I didn't mind doing these things because he was deeply in debt, and I wanted us to start our married life free from financial entanglements.

He did indeed begin a marriage out of debt, only it was with someone else. Two weeks before our wedding date, he broke our engagement, leaving me with an unused wedding gown, shattered dreams, two nonrefundable tickets to Hawaii, and a receipt for a paid hotel room in Honolulu. He also left me several thousand dollars poorer, money with which he paid all his bills and bought a new car. The IRS later slapped my other cheek when they informed me that I owed $12,000 in taxes. I couldn't laugh for crying. The same day I received the news concerning my tax problem, I had $3.32 in my bank account. I must admit I got a lot of practice in the grace of forgiveness each time I drove to my second job and saw my former fiancé in his new car with his new bride. He has not repaid me, nor has he even acknowledged the debt.

The devastation that hit me was so ruinous that were it not for Chris I probably would have walked away. The grace of God and the wise counsel and love of friends sustained me, and both the pain of rejection and the mountainous financial debt have vanished.

In the fall of 1986 the law school at Oral Roberts University transferred to CBN University. One day early in 1987 a handsome student in that school sat next to me in a university chapel service. Following the program, we began a conversation that has not yet ended.

# Conclusion

I have not sought to present myself as a worthy example of persevering faith and certainly not as a perfect model of virtuous womanhood. I claim to be nothing more than what I am—one whom God loved enough to salvage from a ruinous lifestyle and to recreate her, causing old things to pass away and everything to become new (2 Cor. 5:17). So, while in the natural I may well be a daughter of deceit, in reality I am a child of God, His heir, and a fellow heir with Christ (Rom 8:16–17). That lofty status was granted to me by God's grace, which I received through faith in Jesus Christ. Anyone who exercises like faith may also realize the same blessing.

As I have painfully related in the preceding pages, my life has been anything but cushy, even after I became a Christian. Just like the character Much-Afraid in Hannah Hurnard's allegory, *Hinds' Feet on High Places*, my companions were Sorrow and Suffering. But at the end of each trial they became Joy and Peace. The Bible promises that "we can rejoice . . . when we run into problems and trials for we know that they are good for us—they help us learn to be patient. And patience develops strength of character in us and helps us trust God more each time we use it until finally our hope and faith are strong and steady. When that happens, we are able to hold our heads high no matter what happens and know that all is well, for we know how dearly God loves us and we feel this warm love everywhere within us because God has given us the Holy Spirit to fill our hearts with his love" (Rom. 5:3–5).

Therefore, on the basis of my own experience and in light of biblical teachings, I can assure people struggling with circumstances beyond their abilities that God is faithful to deliver, and hope in Him never disappoints. Please don't grow discouraged if that deliverance seems to be delayed; God's timing is perfect. I waited three years for the return

of my son, and the last two years of that period were spent
in eager expectation of the fulfillment of a prophecy that
assured me that Chris and I would be reunited. When I first
heard that word, I thought its fulfillment would be
immediate. It was not easy to maintain hope when months
passed with nothing but a wider distance between me and
my son and harsher privations in my personal existence.
Against all odds, I believed and am still reaping the benefits.
Don't give up!

I call upon all parents to put the needs of their children
before their own interests. Particularly I warn against greed
and the abuses that spring from it. My father was so consumed
with insatiable greed that he sacrificed his family to satisfy his
lusts. It was a terrible price to pay, not only for himself and
the others involved with him but for the rest of us who were
destroyed as a family and marred as individuals. The Bible
declares that the sins of the father affect his descendants to
the fourth generation (Exod. 20:5; 34:7; et al.), a sad
testimony to the fact that no man sins alone. Self-indulgence is
frightfully expensive, and parents who deviate from the
biblical pattern of rearing children "in the discipline and
instruction of the Lord" (Eph. 6:4 NASB) are guilty of
disgraceful neglect.

I grieve deeply for my father and continue to pray for him.
Although I strongly desire to have regular contact with him,
he will not respond to any overtures I make. In order for our
relationship to be restored, he must be willing for a healing to
begin. Unfortunately, to this point he has refused to have
anything to do with me. The tragedy of the whole sordid
business is that John Walker, being deceived by a lie as old as
the beginning of mankind, traded so much for so little. He
was deceived into thinking that he deserved whatever he
thought would satisfy him and that no restraints—legal,
domestic, or spiritual—should be allowed to deter him from
his pursuits. Now he has nothing but a shameful legacy.

With the remote possibility that my father may read this
book, I extend this personal message to him:

Dad, I offer no apology to you for the part I played in your apprehension, because the terrible wrong in which you were involved has ceased. My prayer is that your imprisonment will prove to be your liberation as you reflect upon your life as it has been and can yet be. I can vividly recall what you once were and long to see you realize your full potential as an individual endowed with multiple gifts from God. Even now those abilities can be channeled in a direction that will honor God and bless many people, foremost among whom can be your own family.

Please don't let your pride keep you from the joy of giving and receiving forgiveness. I forgive you for the wrongs you inflicted upon me, and I ask you to forgive me for not being the daughter I should have been. Is there any way I could have been the key to the contented life that you were looking for and couldn't find? I have not told you that I love you since you rejected me as a child. Now, regardless of your feelings toward me, I want you to know that I do love you unconditionally.